I0638020

2017 | Issue #1

U.P. READER

Bringing Upper Michigan Literature to the World

A publication of the Upper Peninsula
Publishers and Authors Association (UPPAA)
Marquette, Michigan

MODERN
HISTORY
PRESS

Castle Rock, St. Ignace - 1920

U.P. Reader: Bringing Upper Michigan Literature to the World -- Issue #1

Learn more about the UPPAA at www.UPPAA.org
Visit UP Reader online at www.UPReader.org

ISSN: 2572-0961
ISBN 978-1-61599-336-9 paperback
ISBN 978-1-61599-337-6 eBook

Managing Editor - Mikel B. Classen
Associate Editor and Copy Editor - Deborah K. Frontiera
Logistical Support & Website Creation - Victor R. Volkman
Cover Photo "Freighter and Moon" - Mikel B. Classen
Cover Design – Doug West
Interior Layout – Michal Šplho, Design Amorandi

Distributed by Ingram (USA/CAN/AU), Bertram's Books (UK/EU)

Published by
Modern History Press
5145 Pontiac Trail
Ann Arbor, MI 48105

www.ModernHistoryPress.com
info@ModernHistoryPress.com

CONTENTS

Introduction

by Mikel B. Classen

◆❖◆

When we came up with the idea for the *U.P. Reader*, we wanted to create a forum for authors from the Upper Peninsula Publishers and Authors Association where we could showcase the talent within the organization and promote their writing. We put out a call for material and we received some of the best. This volume is the result of some of the incredible writing talent we have within the UPPAA.

Filled with stories and poetry, this first volume took on a life of its own. The submissions that came in started to show the real potential of what this project could be. We were pleasantly surprised at the high quality of writing that appeared with every submission. We knew we had some excellent potential out there, but to see it come in first hand was a real treat.

What you hold in your hand is the result of this writing "experiment." The U.P Reader, Issue #1, has exceeded all of our expectations. And we hope it will exceed yours. Enjoy some of the finest Yooper writing ever placed between pages in the premier issue of *U.P. Reader*.

I really need to thank Deborah Frontiera for editing, helping with submissions and making sure that info about the project got out to the membership as well as moral support. I also need to thank Victor Volkman for helping with graphics and getting the *U.P. Reader* into print. This would not have been done without him. I need to thank Tyler Tichelaar and the UPPAA board for believing in the project and making it a reality. And most of all I want to thank the contributors without whom none of this would be possible.

Enjoy!

Mikel B. Classen –
Managing Editor

Loading copper ingots, Houghton

The Song of Minnehaha

by Larry Buege

"Sean, I went to town for groceries. I'll be back by noon. There's a breakfast burrito in the freezer. Nuke it for two minutes. And don't forget your insulin, ten units of regular and twenty of Lente."

Never marry a nurse; they always treat you like a patient. I've been taking insulin for twenty years. One would think that would suggest a modicum of medical knowledge. Despite her occasional nagging, Clara has been a good wife. I write, "I'll be in the woods when you return," at the bottom of Clara's note and leave it on the kitchen table. My penmanship has never been great; now, with the arthritis in my hands, it is barely legible.

I walk over to the fridge and remove the vial of regular insulin; I won't need the Lente today. The breakfast burrito also does not fit my plans. I place the insulin in a plastic grocery bag and head for the den.

We've been spending summers in this cabin overlooking Lake Superior for thirty years. It is no longer a second home; for me, it is home. This is where I found motivation to write. Some of my best works owe their conception to a small spark of inspiration gleaned from these forty acres of Upper Peninsula wilderness.

Most of the cabin belongs to Clara, but the den is mine. It is small, to be sure, but it provides my basic needs. The fabric on my red sofa is worn and frayed. If Clara had her way, it would have been banished to sofa heaven years ago. (It has too many memories for me to discard.) Up against the window overlooking Lake Superior is my oak desk. This is where I did my writing, first on a manual typewriter and then by computer. I say that in past tense since my arthritis prevents all but the most essential writing. Now, only my dictionary and thesaurus remain on the desk. They were my workhorses, receiving extensive use as I searched for that elusive stronger verb or that more descriptive noun. Samuel Clemens purportedly said, "The difference between the right word and the almost right word is the difference between lightning and a lightning bug." Sam was a wise man.

The walls are covered with knotty pine, although bookshelves and pictures obscure much of it. Most of the pictures I took myself: local landscapes and spring flowers. One picture is of a much younger me accepting a Pulitzer Prize for my fifth novel. I find that a bit vain, but Clara insists it remains on the wall.

The bookshelves are where I store my memories and contain the more important books I have read over the years. Even now, as I look at the titles and then close my eyes, I can replay the stories in vivid detail. My memory is one of the few physical attributes that has not exsanguinated with age. My other senses have been relegated to the endangered species list. Despite three laser surgeries, doctors predict diabetes will claim my eyesight within a year.

Twenty-three books on the shelf have my name on the spine. I hope that is a worthy legacy of my life. It is a silly thing for an old man to think about. I pull an old, leather-bound book from the top shelf and add it to the insulin in my plastic bag. Of all the books on the shelf, this is the book I hold in highest esteem—even above those I have authored. I close the door to the den behind me and exit the cabin through the back door.

It will be a warm day. The matutinal sun is already above the trees, suffusing the clearing in which the cabin stands with sunlight. The radiant warmth feels good on my skin. I head down a well-worn path into the woods, a trip I make daily in the summer. The path is lined on both sides by trilliums, a sure sign of spring. It is one of nature's eternal truths; trilliums will be blooming in spring thousands of years after maggots have finished dining on my remains. About one hundred yards into the woods, the path opens into a clearing of sorts. The trees still provide a canopy overhead, but the ground has been cleared of underbrush, revealing a small brook. It is too small to qualify as a stream or even a creek. It is only two feet across at its widest spot and in the dry summer months is almost non-existent. The brook drains down from the hill above the cabin and culminates in a gentle waterfall of no more than three feet in height. The water gurgles as it cascades from one rock to the next.

I sit down on a reclining lawn chair I keep there for that purpose; even the short walk from the cabin leaves me tired. I write in my den, but this is where I think. The formula for a good novel, I have discovered, is two parts thinking and one part writing. I take the insulin from the bag and draw up 100 units; I assume that will be sufficient. Then I inject it into the subcutaneous tissue of my belly. I do not bother with the perfunctory alcohol swab.

I take the book out of the bag and caress the aged leather binding. Books have been my life, my sole reason for existence. That had not always been the case. I close my eyes and remember that summer day in 1954. The war in Korea had ended and times were good. I remember standing before that square edifice of red brick and stone that squatted on a small knoll overlooking Union Street. Its windows were tall and slender and arched at the top like a cathedral. Their lower ledges were well over six feet tall, precluding any thought of peering in—not that I cared to—and the door to the building was recessed in a cave-like structure covered by a high, vaulted arch of cut stone. A drawbridge would not have been out of place. Above the arch, etched in sandstone, was Carnegie Public Library, Sparta, Michigan.

I had walked past the building on my way to school, but I had never been inside. I had walked past many buildings on my way to school, none as formidable as that stone fortress now peering down on me. No other building so totally dominated the landscape or so filled me with trepidation.

School was out for the summer, and fifth grade wouldn't begin until fall; I could find no logical reason for my being there. Summers were for fun and excitement. I should be standing on the pitcher's mound, throwing fastballs in Little League and bowing to cheering crowds. Someday I would stand on the pitcher's mound at Tiger Stadium. When I closed my eyes, I could hear the roar of the crowd as my fastball whipped over the plate for strike three. This was not to be; a cast on my right wrist prohibited any fastballs. I was out for the season.

With the summer in ruins and nothing significant to occupy my time, I had been relegated to errand boy, returning a library book for my mother. It was a degrading chore at best: books were for girls; baseball was for boys. My mother asked that I personally give the book to Mrs. Weaver, one of the librarians and a close friend of my mother's. According to my mother, Mrs. Weaver was a full-blooded Ojibway. Weaver didn't sound very Indian to me.

Once I was assured none of my friends was watching, I slipped into the library. The inside was smaller than I had imagined. It was one large room with rows of bookshelves lined up like fields of corn. They were so tall I would have been unable to reach the top shelf, if for some unforeseen circumstance the need should arise. In the center, sitting at a large oak desk, guarding the books, was an elderly lady with hair that was not gray, but white like freshly fallen snow, and it billowed up in a bun like a snowdrift. Her skin was unusually tanned for this early in the summer. Hanging around her neck by a chain was a pair of turtle-shell glasses, a fitting accouterment to her profession. The name plaque on her desk identified her as Minne Weaver.

"Mrs. Weaver?" I said as I cautiously approached the desk as one would a trial judge.

She looked up and scrutinized all four-foot-two of me, paying particular attention to the flaming red hair protruding from under my Detroit Tigers baseball cap. "You must be Sean Connolly. I talked to your mother yesterday."

We had not previously met, but with my red hair, I was not difficult to pick out of a crowd. As the summer progressed, my face would be covered with freckles. The red hair I could tolerate; the freckles I could do without.

"Are you really an Indian?" I asked. "You don't look like an Indian." My mother would have been horrified by my question, but it was something any ten-year-old would need to know.

"You don't look much like Daniel Boone either," she replied. "You're thinking of historical Indians like you see in the movies." She opened her purse and pulled out a well-worn picture. "This is my grandfather."

I looked at the man in the black and white photo. He had dark skin and high cheekbones, and his hair was black with braids on both sides. Although he was wearing an old-style, tailored suit, he was very much an Indian. I could visualize him riding scout for John Wayne.

"There are many Indians in the Upper Peninsula where I grew up," she said. "My husband and I married after college. John worked for the mines as a geologist. When he died four years ago, I moved down here to work in the library."

Her eyes began to water—old people tend to get sentimental at times. I felt bad; I had only wanted to know if she was Indian. She grabbed a tissue from her desk and dabbed her eyes dry as if no explanation were needed.

"My mother asked me to return this book." I laid the book on her desk, hoping the distraction would alleviate her sorrow.

She checked the due date and set the book on a rolling cart half filled with books. Then she gave my red hair and cap another once-over. "You must be a Tigers fan."

"Yes, ma'am. I'm going to play for the Detroit Tigers when I grow up. My uncle promised to take me to one of their games when he comes home from Korea." I looked down self-consciously at the cast on my wrist. "I fell off my friend's horse a couple of weeks ago and broke my wrist. I'd be playing ball now if it weren't for this." I held up my cast as exhibit "A".

"That can happen to any ballplayer. Even Casey had his bad days."

"Casey? Who'd he play for?" I had baseball cards for Babe Ruth, Ty Cobb, Mickey Mantle, and all the baseball greats, but I couldn't remember anyone named Casey. He had to be a minor leaguer.

"You never heard of Mighty Casey of the Mudville Nine?"

I felt a bit of shame. "No, ma'am."

"We need to correct that. I'll be right back." The lady disappeared into the cornfields and reappeared with a well-worn book. "Take this home and read 'Casey at the Bat' on page 29." She handed me the book. The title of the book was *The Best of American Poetry*. I felt trapped. The noose was tightening around my neck and the trap door quivered beneath my feet. I couldn't just give the book back to her.

"Just make sure you return it in two weeks."

I left the library with the book of poetry under my shirt. If any of my friends were to see it, I'd never survive the razzing... and poetry of all books. Ten years old and my manhood was already in question. I gave the baseball field a wide berth to avoid any encounters with close friends and arrived home with my pride intact. I yelled a quick "hello" to my mother, who was fixing dinner in the kitchen, and headed upstairs to my room. I didn't feel safe until my bedroom door was securely closed behind me. I would hide the book under my mattress and smuggle it back into the library the following morning. No one would be the wiser.

Before Mighty Casey was sequestered in the safety of my mattress, I had to see who he was. I turned to page 29, finding "Casey at the Bat" by Ernest Lawrence Thayer.

The outlook wasn't brilliant for the Mudville nine that day.

The score stood four to two, with but one inning more to play,

And then when Cooney died at first, and Barrows did the same,

A pall-like silence fell upon the patrons of the game.

The legendary Harry Caray couldn't have better described the game. I continued reading down the page, fascinated with the rhythm of the story. It was as if I were there or at least listening to the play-by-play description on the radio. I had no doubt Mighty Casey would save the day.

Oh, somewhere in this favored land the sun is shining bright,

The band is playing somewhere, and somewhere hearts are light,

And somewhere men are laughing, and little children shout;

But there is no joy in Mudville? Mighty Casey has struck out.

The ending was a letdown; I had wanted Casey to clear the bases. This was unlike any poetry I had ever read. There was no flowery language or mushy romance. It was a poem a boy could read without shame, not that I planned to tell anyone. I scanned the table of contents but found no more baseball poems. "The Midnight Ride of Paul Revere" piqued my interest; I liked horses. I turned to page 89.

Listen my children and you shall hear

Of the midnight ride of Paul Revere,

For the next few minutes I rode "through every Middlesex village and farm, for the country folk to be up and to arm." I could feel the wind in my face as my trusty steed galloped through the countryside. The horse's mane stung as it whipped across my cheek, but I didn't care. I rode through Lexington and on to Concord, all the time yelling, "The British are coming! The British are coming!" Finding nothing more of interest in the book, I stashed it under my mattress.

I returned to the library the following morning, my book safely tucked under my shirt. Mrs. Weaver was sitting at her desk overlooking her domain. I assumed defending her desk against all comers was part of her job description.

"Good morning, Mrs. Weaver. I'm returning your book."

"What did you think of 'Casey at the Bat'?"

"It was O.K., I guess. Is he a real person?"

"He can be if you want him to. Did you read any other poems?"

I wondered if conversations with librarians were privileged like talking to a priest or an attorney. "I read about Paul Revere."

"Ah, Longfellow, one of my favorite poets. Let me show you something."

She reached into one of her desk drawers and pulled out a brown paper bag. Inside was a book aged by time. It was bound in brown leather and trimmed in gold leaf. For a moment I feared she was going to pawn another book on me.

"This is one of the earliest editions of Longfellow's *Song of Hiawatha*. I'm told it's worth a lot of money—not that I would ever sell it. It tells about the adventures of a young Indian boy about your age named Hiawatha. Longfellow personally gave it to my grandfather." She opened it to the first page. "See." I looked at the page and saw Henry Wadsworth Longfellow scribbled in the margin. "My grandfather gave it to my mother, and she gave it to me. I had hoped to pass it on to my son or daughter, but John and I never had any children." Her eyes began to water again. She seemed to get teary-eyed every time she talked about her husband.

She opened the book to one of the earlier pages. "Listen to this: By the shores of Gitche Gumee by the shining Big-Sea-Water stood the wigwam of Nokomis."

"What's gitche gumee?"

"That's the Ojibway name for Lake Superior, where I grew up. Longfellow uses a lot of Indian names." She closed the book and carefully returned it to her paper bag. "Most people call me Minne, but my real name is Minnehaha. My mother named me after Hiawatha's lover. Minnehaha means waterfall in Dakota."

"Does the book have any horses in it?"

"I don't believe so. You like horses?"

"Yes, ma'am. I have a friend who lives on a horse farm. We ride them sometimes. That's how I broke my wrist. The horse got spooked and I fell off. It wasn't his fault."

"You fell off a horse and broke your wrist and you still like horses?"

"Yes, ma'am. When you fall off a horse you got to get right back on. Mom won't let me ride until the cast comes off, but then I'm going to get right back on that horse."

"You remind me of Alec Ramsay."

"Who's he?"

"He's a boy a bit older than you but has your red hair and freckles. He has his very own horse."

"Wow, I wish I had my own horse."

"If I remember right, Alec spent the summer with his uncle who was a missionary in India. On returning home, his ship sank in a storm. Luckily for Alec, the ship had a wild horse onboard. Both Alec and the horse were thrown overboard. Alec grabbed the rope tied around the horse's neck, and the horse pulled him to the safety of a small island. No one survived the shipwreck to claim the horse, so the horse became Alec's."

"Some people have all the luck. Nothing that exciting ever happens to me. Does Alec live around here?"

"Yes, I believe he does…. Let me check."

Mrs. Weaver slowly walked over to one of the stacks as if each step inflicted considerable pain. I hadn't noticed that before. I assumed she had arthritis. A lot of old folks did. She returned with a book in hand, obviously for me—she had tricked me again.

"This is *The Black Stallion* by Walter Farley. I think you'll like it," she said. She gave me the book, which I was obliged to take. "Make sure you return it in two weeks."

"Yes, ma'am," I said.

I returned home with the book again hidden under my shirt and immediately took it to my room. Out of curiosity, I flipped through the pages. Scattered among the sheets of prose were drawings in black ink. One showed a black horse rearing up on its hind legs. The horse had bulging muscles that rippled and gleamed like those of a prizefighter. He was sleek and mean-looking, not the kind of horse that would tolerate a saddle.

I opened to the first page: *The tramp steamer Drake plowed away from the coast of India and pushed its blunt prow into the Arabian Sea…* I was on page 14 when my mother called me for dinner. The Drake was in a terrible storm and had been struck by lightning; it was beginning to sink. People were heading toward the lifeboats; the situation didn't look good.

After supper I asked to be excused so I could organize my baseball cards. It was not an unusual request; I often spent many hours with my baseball cards. I felt bad about the lie, but there was no way I could leave Alec in the middle of that storm with the ship sinking. I read well into the evening.

In the summer my parents let me stay up until ten o'clock. By then the Black Stallion had dragged Alec to a small deserted island, undoubtedly saving his life, but the Black Stallion was still a wild beast capable of killing Alec at any moment.

"Sean, time to turn off the lights."

I looked at the clock on my dresser. It was hard to believe it was already ten. I dog-eared my page and placed the book in its secure spot under my mattress. I turned off the light and lay in bed wondering how Alec would survive on the island without food and water. Finally, I could endure no more. I found a flashlight in my closet and crawled under the covers so my parents wouldn't see my light shining on the ground from their bedroom window, and I read late into the night. When I awoke in the morning, the batteries to my flashlight were dead. The book lay on the floor with a dog-ear marking the place I had stopped. I finished the book in two days.

I found Mrs. Weaver sitting at her desk as usual, the desk piled high with stacks of books. I placed *The Black Stallion* on a vacant spot on her desk. "I enjoyed the book," I said.

She looked up at me and smiled as if she knew I would. "He's quite the horse, isn't he?"

"Even with his cut foot, he beat both Sun Raider and Cyclone. The race wasn't even close."

"He also won the Kentucky Derby," Mrs. Weaver added.

"No, ma'am," I said. "The race was in Chicago." I hated to correct her, but she was clearly mistaken.

"That was the race against Sun Raider and Cyclone. You don't think the Black Stallion stopped racing after Chicago, do you?"

She must have seen the confusion on my face. "Follow me," she said. She picked up *The Black Stallion* and headed toward the cornfield, walking slowly, obviously in pain. She stopped at an aisle labeled *Juvenile* and headed down the row, stopping midway down the aisle. "These are the *F*s," she said. "The books are in alphabetical order by the author's last name. All these books were written by Walter Farley." She returned *The Black Stallion* to the stack.

I looked at the books in amazement. There were *The Black Stallion Returns, Son of the Black Stallion, The Black Stallion Revolts, The Black Stallion Mystery*. There must have been fifteen or more books in all.

"Walter Farley wrote a whole series about the Black Stallion." She pulled out *The Black Stallion Returns*. "This is the second book in the series."

"Can I read that one?" I asked.

She gave me the book. "Bring it back in two weeks."

I left the library with my treasure firmly gripped in my hands. I didn't care who saw me. I would read every one of the Black Stallion books; I had all summer. I finished reading The *Black Stallion Returns* in three days and returned for another book. Each time I read a book, Mrs. Weaver would quiz me about the story. I didn't need much encouragement; I was always willing to tell her about Alec's adventures.

Summer passed by too quickly. By late August I had read eight of the books. With two weeks left before school started, it seemed unlikely I would complete the series. Homework would make finding time for reading difficult. With *The Black Stallion Revolts* under my arm, I walked into the library. It was unusually quiet even for a library. I walked over to the main desk. Instead of Mrs. Weaver, a man in his late forties was sitting at her desk. I felt a bit of anger; he had no right to be there. That was Mrs. Weaver's desk.

"Where's Mrs. Weaver?" I demanded as if the man had personally hidden her away somewhere.

The man looked up at me, paying particular attention to the red hair under my Detroit Tigers' baseball cap. "Mrs. Weaver died last night," he said, choosing his words carefully. "She had cancer, you know. She had been in a lot of pain."

I was overcome with shock. What the man was telling me couldn't be true. I wanted to run out of the library and never come back, but my feet wouldn't respond. I just stared at the man in disbelief.

"You must be Sean Connolly."

"Yes, sir."

"Mrs. Weaver spoke very highly of you." He reached into Mrs. Weaver's desk drawer and pulled out a package. It was wrapped in plain brown paper and had a card taped to the outside. "She wanted you to have this."

I thanked the man and quickly left the library; I didn't want anyone to see me cry, but I cried all the way home. I went straight to my room so my mother wouldn't see the tears in my eyes. I set the package on my bed, preferring not to open it as if opening the package would somehow confirm Mrs. Weaver's death. Then, I cried quietly for another ten minutes. She had given me a new life filled with fun and adventure, and now she had taken it away. It wasn't right.

The card attached to the package said simply, "Sean Connolly." I removed the card from the package—my mother always insisted I read the card first. I recognized Mrs. Weaver's meticulous handwriting. She wrote with a flourish that made me envious. My teachers always told me my handwriting left something to be desired.

"When you read this you will know that I am gone," she wrote. "Summer went by too quickly, but you made my last days enjoyable. Please don't cry for me. I am happy now, for I am Minnehaha the waterfall, and I must return to my homeland. I have gone to join my Hiawatha, and together we shall walk along the shores of Gitche Gumee by

VIEW OF THE TOWN OF MACKINAW.

City of Mackinaw engraving - 1850

the shining Big-Sea-Water. If you come to visit, which I hope you do, you will find me in the mournful cry of the loon or the chirp of the cricket or the susurration of the gentle waterfall. I will be there for you."

I set the card aside, my eyes still filled with tears. I would never read another book without thinking of her. I knew what it was before I opened the package and pulled out the book. It was bound in aged brown leather and decorated with gold leaf. On the cover, printed in gold leaf, was—*The Song of Hiawatha.*

I caress the old leather binding with tired, arthritic fingers as I have done so many times in the past. Even with my eyes closed, I can identify every crease, every imperfection, as if such a book could have imperfections. The book has lost none of its magic over the years. Just holding it gives me an ineffable pleasure that even I cannot express in words.

Around me crickets are chirping, and down by the lake, a loon is voicing its lonely, mournful cry. The day is becoming cool. I feel a chill cut through my body, although a sheen of sweat covers my skin. I try to lift my hand to my throbbing head, but lack the strength. Vaguely I feel each heartbeat pounding within my chest, as adrenaline tries to compensate for the lack of glucose flowing in my blood. My heart races. It is a race it cannot win. My thoughts begin to fog. Where am I? I wonder. The crickets have ceased their chirping, as if to observe a moment of silence, and I can no longer hear the loon down by the lake. All I hear is the susurration of a gentle waterfall—and then there is silence.

Larry Buege's short stories have received regional and international (English) awards. He has also authored eight novels including the ever-popular Chogan Native American series. More information about his novels can be found at Gastropodpublishing.com or by contacting the author directly at LSBuege@aol.com.

Fragile Blossoms

by Deborah K. Frontiera

Fragile blossoms burst
Brief fireworks of life in spite
Of jagged rough rocks

Nature, especially in the sometimes harsh environment of Michigan's Upper Peninsula, often reminds us of our place within the system and our responsibility to the planet we live on. Wild flowers live such short, but beautiful, lives giving us joy during the brief months when there is no snow on the ground. They also remind us that on this planet, no matter how strong we might think we are, the system of life on Earth is equally fragile. It is our responsibility to live within it wisely or we may disappear as quickly as flowers die after an early frost or when battered by strong winds and waves.

Deborah K. Frontiera, who grew up in Michigan's Upper Peninsula, has lived in Houston, TX, since 1985, and taught in Houston Independent School District until 2008. Three of her books have been honor or award winners. She has published fiction, nonfiction, and poetry for all ages in both books and periodicals. She is a migratory creature, returning to her beloved U.P. every spring—rather like the Canada geese, millions of which spend their winters on the Katy Prairie just west of Houston, TX.

Visit her website at: www.authorsden.com/deborahkfrontiera.

Winning Ticket

by James M. Jackson

Winter light leaking through the crescent window above the door did little to brighten the kitchen. Depressing, Sheriff Edward Sinclair thought, just to stand here. What must it be to live in one of these cookie-cutter apartment buildings with their dilapidated exteriors and shabby furnishings? Would he fall this low—a kitchen lit by a bare forty-watt bulb over the card table? He leaned his six-two, linebacker frame gone flaccid against the kitchen wall and patted his pockets for a cigarette before remembering he'd left them in the car. He needed to move this confrontation along.

"Your choice," Sinclair said and gave a single-shoulder shrug. "Leave the county by Christmas or press your claim for the *Megabuck$* four million dollars and go to jail."

"No fair," sputtered Wayne Waverly. Veins and arteries popped in the bantam's neck; a purple line on his forehead throbbed with his rapid heartbeat. "You're the chief of police. You can't shake me down."

"What's not fair is what your fake lottery tickets did to people's hopes. You should have seen how ecstatic my maid, Juanita, was this morning after she found a ticket at Horvath's Cleaners. It crushed her when I told her it was worthless." He pushed off the wall, straightened his tired back, and glared down at Waverly. "If it weren't the holiday season, you'd be in cuffs right now."

"I'll squeal to the papers. I bought that ticket. I played those numbers for the last six months." Spittle flecked his speech. He pointed at Sinclair. "You know that's the truth."

"Who's going to believe a two-time loser who violated parole scattering forged winning lottery tickets around town? You're the Grinch, the stealer of American dreams. You didn't even perpetrate your hoax to make money. No, you just wanted everyone else to be as miserable as you are. You're disgusting." Sinclair flashed a capped-tooth smile. "Besides, they trust me, everyone's favorite chief."

Waverly plopped onto the cracked plastic of the lone kitchen chair. Spreading his hands in front of him, he said, "Hows about we split the money once the real ticket shows? You said yourself I can prove it's mine."

"Except, you got nothing. *You* gave *me* the evidence. Remember? It's not my fault you gave away the winning ticket and kept one of your fakes." Sinclair shot back his French cuffs and fussed at checking his Rolex to add some nonverbal pressure. "Which is it? Walk away or enjoy the seven years remaining on your parole for check kiting in a prison of the judge's choice? Plus," he paused until Waverly looked into his eyes, "whatever sentence the judge gives for the forgeries. A three-time loser at forty-five, you'll be eligible for Medicare when you get out. You already got a cauliflower ear from your last incarceration. What's four million worth if you come out in a pine box? Oh, that's right. They don't use wood anymore—a cardboard box."

Waverly slammed out of the chair, grabbed a beer from the refrigerator, and slumped back down at the table, his energy spent. Between slugs he appeared engaged in a silent argument with himself, eyes shifting from right to left and back.

Sinclair ambled away from the table and leaned against the door, hoping the stench of ancient grease wouldn't permeate his camelhair coat. How could anyone put up with peeling putrid-green paint and cracked, yellowed linoleum floors? Yet in three days—the 27th—the bank would foreclose Sinclair's house. Then where would he be?

Sinclair waited. Even Waverly's pea brain would soon realize his only real choice was to pack his computer equipment and go.

The duty sergeant had suggested Sinclair's grandfatherly style might work best with a crank who claimed someone stole his winning ticket. People acted strange during the holidays, and Sinclair's policy encouraged departmental leniency, particularly on Christmas Eve day. So, Sinclair made the call intending Christmas kindness.

Waverly's name hadn't registered, but once Sinclair saw his face, he remembered the parolee. To Sinclair's surprise, the claim was legit. But in proving his case, Waverly had invited him into the bedroom with all the computer gear and coughed up evidence of the forged lottery tickets.

If Sinclair could find the real winning ticket, it would solve his financial problems once he got Waverly out of the way.

"I ain't going back," Waverly finally said.

"Good thinking. Shouldn't have any trouble finding these luxury accommodations in the next county or two or three. Just remember to stay in state or your parole's toast."

"Whole damned world's been against me since I was born," Waverly muttered. Looking up at Sinclair he said, "Can I at least look for it?"

Sinclair knew he had won. "And say what? 'Hi. Did you find one of my fake tickets in a red and green envelope with Merry Christmas on the front?' You crazy? You'd be lynched."

Waverly finished his beer and got another. "All right, I'm leaving."

"Then stop drinking. You don't want to get busted for DUI." Sinclair levered his shoulder off the door, walked to Waverly, and offered his hand. "Good decision. You got tonight and tomorrow to get your stuff out of here. I see you after Christmas, I'll bust your butt. Good luck."

Waverly stared at the proffered hand and drained his beer.

• • •

Sinclair spent the rest of the afternoon in his headquarters' office aimlessly moving paper from one pile to another, raiding the plates of cookies and tins of nuts left by well-meaning citizens, not tasting their staleness or registering that someone had snuck in rum balls again this year. He flashed his smile and called out "Merry Christmas" to the clerks and officers as they left for Christmas Eve. Everyone was in a good mood, and he was glad he could stop faking it when the last deputy, other than the lone dispatcher on duty, finally left.

With a sigh, he stacked the papers into his in-basket, locked his door, and walked through the deserted office, turning off the lighted Christmas tree and smiling Santa. Wrinkling his nose at the pizza boxes discarded from lunch, he slipped through the break room and down the back stairway. In the evidence room, he removed all the "winning" tickets turned in that week by citizens in their zeal to catch the hoax's perpetrator. Sinclair slipped the evidence into his briefcase and returned upstairs. He passed the dispatcher on his way out and said, "Merry Christmas. Hope Santa's good to you and yours."

On his way home, he drove past Waverly's place. The single light in the kitchen showed the shotgun apartment was empty. He'd soon find out if the gamble had paid off.

• • •

Sinclair sat at the antique cherry desk in his study and examined each ticket with a magnifying glass. None exhibited the minute markings Waverly had shown him a real ticket would have. He returned all the files to evidence bags.

At Juanita's distinctive knock, he shoved the evidence into his briefcase and pulled a file from the center drawer. Bad choice, he thought, after his eye caught the title of the legal document: PROPOSED FORE-

CLOSURE—DECEMBER 27. The house had been in his wife's family almost 150 years. What would he tell their children? Before summoning Juanita, he snapped off the latex gloves he'd worn to protect the evidence and stubbed out the English Oval in the overflowing ashtray.

She eased open the chestnut pocket doors. Even wearing thick sandals, her lithe frame barely reached five feet. Her alert black eyes scanned the room and, as always, a smile highlighted her oval face.

"Pardon, Señor." Even though she'd emigrated from Guatemala four years ago, she still pronounced *d* as a *th*. "Before I go, I want to make sure you okay." She opened the window a crack. "Too much smoke. Not good for you. I come tomorrow. You want?"

"No, no. No work on Christmas. You have a wonderful day. I'll be fine."

"I be home if you need." She pointed to the carriage house. "I leave you tomorrow food. You can microwave?"

Sinclair reached into his right top drawer and pulled out an envelope. "Here." He couldn't look her in the eye as he handed her the envelope stuffed with crisp twenty-dollar bills. "A Christmas present. You've taken such good care of me and the house since my wife died."

"*Mucho gracias, Señor.*" She bowed her head and looked at the polished oak floor. "I make present for you." She reached into her apron pocket, pulled out a small wooden box, and handed it to Sinclair.

He examined the red and green etchings in the wood, rotating the box to view all six sides.

"Open. No wait 'til later."

He pried off the lid. Small bits of paper and cloth were wound together inside.

"Worry dolls," Juanita said. "Your eyes tell on you. You not sleep good. Before you go to bed, you tell each one a different trouble, and they go away."

Sinclair looked at them with blank eyes.

"Really, *Señor.* You see."

"Thank you, Juanita. Merry Christmas."

She backed out and closed the doors behind her. Sinclair shifted his gaze between the worry dolls and the foreclosure notice.

He'd have no problem finding something to tell each of the dozen dolls.

• • •

Boxing Day: Sinclair's father had celebrated it working in a soup kitchen, his interpretation of the tradition of giving gifts to the lower classes. Today Sinclair would have to tell Juanita he had lost the house and could no longer employ her. Some gift.

The foreclosure file still sat on his desk. He knew its contents by heart, just as he knew the details of the sickening slide of his stock portfolio after his wife's prolonged illness. "Pride goeth before a fall," his mother had always said. If only he hadn't listened to the market guru about it being only a short-term correction—a time for the bold to snap up the bargains. Then he wouldn't have mortgaged the house, lost that money too, and gotten into this fix.

A lead weight had filled his stomach for the last month. He wondered if it would go away once his humiliation was public. Closing the file, he opened the center drawer and spotted the Merry Christmas envelope containing the lottery ticket Juanita had found at Horvath's Cleaners. With a magnifying glass he examined the ticket.

A smile lifted the corners of his mouth and tugged at his eyes. Juanita's dolls *were* magic. Heaving out of the chair, he strode to the back window and surveyed the carriage house, gardens, and rear brick wall, with its ancient wooden gate allowing access to the woods beyond. These grounds were where he felt closest to his wife, dead these two years.

He whistled "In the Bleak Midwinter" and telephoned Jenkins, the president of the bank.

"How soon can you come over?" Sinclair asked. He heard Jenkins's chair creak in protest and pictured him leaning back, staring at the ceiling, measuring his response, balancing the debits and credits of their relationship.

"If it's important," Jenkins stressed the last word, lengthening the middle syllable. "I can be right over."

Voyageurs on Lake Superior at Sunset

"I have extremely good news."

Jenkins released a long sigh. "I'm relieved to hear it."

• • •

"Juanita," Sinclair said. "Please bring two cognacs. The Remy Louis XIII, I think."

Juanita served Jenkins, who had settled his bulk into the leather chair. She laid a coaster on Sinclair's cherry desk and placed his snifter on it.

"Is good?" she asked Sinclair through her smile.

"Perfect. Please stay nearby, we may need you."

Jenkins watched the performance as Juanita backed out of the room. He twirled his cognac, sniffed the bouquet, and aligned his tie so it bisected his girth.

Not a poker player, Sinclair thought. The banker's wide smile gave clear proof Jenkins preferred to avoid foreclosures.

"I'm glad you worked something out," Jenkins said. "Shall I wait for a toast before enjoying this wonder?" He nodded at his glass.

"To winning lottery tickets," Sinclair said, his entire face lifting in a smile. He pulled the ticket worth four million dollars before taxes from the drawer and handed it across the desk.

Jenkins turned it over several times. His face took the look of a plaster death mask. "This isn't some kind of joke is it?"

"It is gen-u-ine."

"That does deserve a good snort." Jenkins took a long swallow. He set his glass down. "You didn't join me. Something else?"

"The ticket belongs to Juanita. She'll need your financial advice before she cashes it in. I'll buzz her and leave you two here to discuss her good fortune."

Sinclair slid out of his chair. "Tomorrow, I'll come to your office."

James M. Jackson authors the Seamus McCree mystery series: *Ant Farm, Bad Policy, Cabin Fever, Doubtful Relations,* and *Empty Promises* (2017). Jim splits his time between the deep woods of Michigan's Upper Peninsula and the open spaces of Georgia's Lowcountry. He is the current president of the 700+ member Guppy Chapter of Sisters in Crime. You can find information about Jim and his books at http://jamesmjackson.com.

Stocking Up

by Janeen Pergrin Rastall

Before the first beech tree decants gold
upon the lawn, collect your summer
memories: scorches on your feet,
your hobble-walk to the water. Gather
green from the fescue. September's gusts
will blanch every blade. Tuck in how
you skip the lawn, scramble from shade lattice
to lattice, how warm berries burst
and cling between your teeth, how bees
displaced by your picking
simmer in hives overhead.
Clump all the moments you can carry,
pack them like a bag during pregnancy, poised
by the door. When January rasps
your cheeks, when the sun
is a tired rind, open up
your summer hoard.

Janeen Pergrin Rastall lives in Gordon, MI (population 2). Janeen is the author of *In the Yellowed House* (dancing girl press 2014), *Objects May Appear Closer* (Celery City Chapbooks, 2015) and co-author of *Heart Radicals* (ELJ Publications, 2016). Her work has been nominated multiple times for a Best of the Net Award and for the Pushcart Prize. Please visit her at her website janeenpergrinrastall.wordpress.com.

We Are Three Widows

by Sharon M. Kennedy

The warm September breeze brings dark, threatening clouds, but no rain comes. I'm glad because I don't want Dad's coffin to get wet before they lower it into his grave. I know if the rain comes no one will tell it from the tears on my cheeks, but still it's important to maintain appearances, at least that's what Mom would say. Appearances must be maintained, even at the burial of a loved one.

I hear the rumble of distant thunder. The gathering green sky is a signal rain isn't far off. I hope the priest shuts up before we all get soaked. His steady, pompous assurance that Dad is in heaven is getting on my nerves. He has no idea where Dad is. Finally, as the first raindrops fall, the priest tells us to go in peace. We bless ourselves, touch the coffin one last time, and hurry to the car. The ride home is quiet except for the steady beat of rain on the windshield and the monotonous slap of the wipers.

We are three widows now. My sister and Mom came by it honestly. I'm divorced but "widow" sounds much better than "divorcee". We are dressed in black, from our pristine veiled hats to our sturdy Red Wing shoes. Dad would have laughed at our getups. He probably would have preferred seeing Mom in a plaid shirt and overalls, MayBeth in a loose fitting blouse and flowered skirt, and me in a brown turtle neck sweater and jeans. Such clothing was representative of our daily wardrobe.

We turn off M-28 towards the side road leading to the house that isn't a house at all, only a trailer. Mom calls it a mobile home, but it's never been home to me. Home was the gray shingled house that came down one night when a wild and furious autumn wind destroyed everything in its wake. I park the car close to the front steps and hurry in before rain spoils our fancy clothes.

Once inside, the wind carries fresh, cold rain through the open windows, and we hurry to close them.

Mom turns to me. "You better bring in Pepper and make sure your bike's in the shed," she says. "I'll get some candles in case the lights go out." She walks down the hall to her bedroom. I watch her disappear and suddenly yearn to be seven again and feel warm and safe in our big, old wooden house. I wasn't afraid when a storm rolled in because I knew my parents and the house would protect me. I knew the maple and poplar trees would stand forever; that Gram would continue knitting by the light of a kerosene lamp if the lights went out; and that Pepper would be safe in the back shed. When I was seven that was the way things were—at least that's how I remembered them. But the maple and poplar rotted away; Pepper's long since dead; Gram's been gone for over 30 years; and my rusty bike went to the junk pile a long time ago.

Mom returns from her room, empty-handed, the candles forgotten. The blank look returns to her face. She hasn't taken off her gloves, and her velvet hat with the spotted veil is still perched on her white hair. Her green eyes go from MayBeth to me. She shakes her head.

"Who are you?" she asks. "And why are you here?" She sits in her plaid rocker and stares at us. Her face is unlined and smooth. Mom is 83, still a pretty woman who never forgets her red lipstick. I look at my sister, but she's thumbing through an issue of *Martha Stewart Living* and ignores me.

"Mom, you know who we are," I say. "I'm Katie and that's MayBeth. We're your daughters." She shakes her head.

"I don't know who you are," she says. "I don't have any daughters. I had a son once, but he died or went away or something. I don't remember all the details." She pets Sweetie, the cat, who has come from her hiding place and curled in Mom's lap.

From a window we neglected to close, a sharp wind blows through the trailer. I turn up the furnace. It rattles to life, clicking and pinging as warm air hits the metal vents. I take the chair next to Mom's and feel the rush of air. As heat fills the room, it blows a thin scarf tied to the floor register. The paisley design dances to life as if some ancient tribal rite has taken possession of the scarf. I watch Mom watching the dance. Her eyes are dry and empty behind her glasses. I can't imagine what emotions pass through her, but I know the ones that pass through me. Sorrow and I are old friends. When the heat shuts off and the dance ends, Mom turns to me.

"Is there any tea?" she asks. I tell her it's almost ready, walk into the kitchen, and pour hot water over a fresh tea bag. I open the refrigerator and reach for a Saran-wrapped salmon sandwich and cut it into four pieces, just the way Mom likes it. I open a box of gingersnap cookies and take some out. I spread butter between them, place them next to the sandwich, and put everything on a black metal tray with a map of Michigan painted on it. "Here, Mom," I say. "Everything's ready." She eats slowly, dabbing at invisible crumbs at the corners of her mouth, then turns to me.

"Say," she says. "You remind me of a girl I once knew. She was a feisty little thing with long brown pigtails and eyes that crossed. I don't remember her name."

I tell her I'm that little girl, but she corrects me.

"No, dear," she says as she takes my hand. "You're an old woman."

A chill steals into my bones. Mom pats my hand then disentangles her fingers from mine. I return to the oak rocker.

The rain has withered to a drizzle, and a whisper of sunlight filters through the lacy ivory curtains. The carpet becomes a soft beige sea beneath my feet. I look around this room at the faces of dead relatives watching me from the confines of their picture frames. A small oak table is cluttered with photographs of relatives I never knew. My eyes rest on Mama's wedding picture. *Mama*. The favored name slips out with the memories.

"It's okay, Mama," I tell her. "Everything's going to be okay. I'll take care of you."

"That's nice," she says, "but I don't need you." Her eyes get that far away look as she pets Sweetie and talks to the cat as if she were speaking to a child.

I return to the kitchen and think. We are three widows, now. We have a bond, a connection that will keep us together. A bond no man can break because the men we loved are gone. The whistle of the tea kettle breaks into my thoughts. "Anyone want more tea?" I ask. But there is no reply. MayBeth has drifted to sleep. Mom is watching the dance of the paisley scarf. I give way to my emotions. Not sadness this time, but acceptance.

It will take a long time for rain to reach Dad's coffin. Somehow that gives me comfort.

Sharon M. Kennedy of Brimley published her book *Life in a Tin Can*, a collection of stories from her newspaper columns. After teaching English Composition at the college level, Sharon returned to her real love. Writing stories that tug at your heartstrings or bring a smile to your lips is her hallmark. She can be reached at P.O. Box 215, Brimley, MI 49715 or https://www.facebook.com/LifeInATinCan

U.P. Road Trips

by Jan Kellis

My Mom was the original girl scout. She never left home without a small jar of matches, a pocket knife, and the book she was currently reading. The trunk of her car contained a shovel, a space blanket, a wine corker, and an axe.

"Have your own," she often said. She believed everyone should be able to support themselves, and save themselves, and take responsibility for their own actions. "And if you say you're going to do something, do it! Don't sit around and make excuses." She believed in self-education (though she had two college degrees), and taught herself everything by reading books. She taught us to do the same.

One of my favorite early memories is of sitting with Mom in the warm slant of the sun, each of us reading our own book and thinking our own thoughts. We did this often.

My memories are like tiny chapter books stored in a jar. These memory books are jammed inside the jar, settled comfortably together, each one protecting its neighbors. Some memory books stay near the center where it's dark, while others seek the light and frequently offer themselves up for review. The earliest memories sank to the bottom long ago. They're fragile and ancient.

They're hardback books, hand-bound, with gold-edged pages. The covers are plain, with simple titles such as *Leaving Home*. If I were to pluck that particular memory book out of its reserved space and open the cover, I would recall everything from the day I packed my worldly belongings into my Ford Pinto and drove away from home. The old-car smell, dust and ancient vinyl and damp carpet, the roll of duct tape gently nudging the gearshift each time I clutched and shifted, and AC/DC caterwauling "Moneytalks". reminding me I had a grand total of $319 saved from several years of babysitting. The music consumed all auditory space, which was my way of ignoring the alarming knocks and squeals emitted by the car. The sun burned my legs through the windshield and my future was shrouded in ever-present anxiety. Back then, I thought ever-present anxiety was normal.

The memory books are like the old scratch-and-sniff stickers, without the scratch; although certain memories do sting a little.

My sister Jen's memory jar isn't as full as mine is because she's seven years less experienced than I am. I sometimes try to add to her jar by relating stories from her toddler years, like the time we took a family vacation in our homemade motorhome when she was two. She doesn't recall my changing the fan belt every 500 miles, which required me to crawl behind the driver's side wheel and reach up into the dirty darkness of the engine. Dad handed me tools while Jen helped Mom make sandwiches for lunch. The memories I toss into her jar aren't complete for her: they arrive without color, sound, or scent, built on flimsy descriptions of events. This is better than nothing.

We have driven across the Upper Peninsula hundreds of times, Jen and I, sometimes together and sometimes apart, and sometimes with other people. East to west and then a bit north, the car always followed the grooves established by our parents and grandparents from one end of M-28 to the other, and part of US41. I always knew when I'd arrived at the family cabin in Eagle River by the scent. Fresh and energetic, with a hint of spruce pitch and nostalgia. Lake Superior set the mood and provided the soundtrack.

The cabin and property have been in our family for six generations, purchased sometime in the late 1800s during the copper boom when our great-great-great-grandfather bought the Eagle River Hotel. When the hotel burned down, the owners pulled the workers' bunkhouses together to form one cabin. According to family lore, it was a temporary shelter to use during the summer. It still stands, a hundred years later, in a glorious slump. It fiercely protects more than twelve decades of family memories.

The last time we drove from east to west and then a bit north, my sister and daughter and I, we barely noticed the small towns and landmarks we breezed by as we spoke of inconsequential things rather than mention the mission we shared. We drove past Hulbert, through MacMillan, through Seney and Shingleton and Champion. The memories lined themselves up along both sides of the road, spines facing the blacktop, guiding us along Mom's preferred route. Here was her favorite beach; there was her favorite restaurant. We sailed past her favorite waterfall trail and through Mohawk and Allouez. The monument bearing our great-great-grandfather's name, John P. Petermann, silently fortified us as we glided by.

We'd picked up a small package, and I drove gently so as not to disturb its contents. What, exactly, is the protocol for handling one's mother's cremated remains? I fought the absurd urge to tuck a book into the bag containing the sacred box so she'd have something to read. I nestled her in the back of the car between our suitcases so nothing would shift or topple during the ride. As usual, she didn't complain.

When we arrived at the cabin, we quickly gathered the items we'd come to retrieve. Car keys, purse, clothes, luggage. We wiped down the kitchen and turned off the water and the power and the propane. We locked the doors.

There were no words.

We walked the beach for a few minutes, letting Mother Superior wash away a fragment of our grief. We'd always been warned about the undertow, and I imagined my despair being tugged out to the depths of the lake.

The week before this grim expedition, we'd had lunch with Mom. She talked about her imminent drive to the cabin, planned for the following day. "It should be a good trip," she'd said. "There are a few miles of road construction on M-28." Like I said, she rarely found fault.

She's the only person I've ever met who enjoyed the scenery along the Seney Stretch. "I like the tamaracks—they're my favorite tree," was her common remark.

Mom passed from this world, into whatever's next, one evening in her favorite place on earth. This was a memory I didn't want in my jar. I covered the opening of the jar with both hands, but the stubborn memory, a thick book with tear-warped pages, appeared in the jar despite my efforts. I wished I could edit my sister's memory book of this unfathomable time and reduce the intensity of it somehow. I wished she could do the same for me.

My sister and daughter followed me in Mom's car as we drove a bit south, then from west to east, all the way back to the easternmost tip of the UP to Mom's beloved Village, where she had raised two daughters to have their own.

Somehow, we withstand the added weight of our memory jars. We are stronger and weaker than we were before.

Jan Stafford Kellis was born reading and started writing soon thereafter. Words continue to fascinate her, and she reads and writes every day. She lives in the eastern end (the best end) of Michigan's Upper Peninsula, where the living is easy and the inspiration is plentiful. Jan has published seven books, including the popular Bookworms Anonymous volumes and three novels. Visit www.jankellis.com to discover the latest news and planned events.

The Story-Seer

by Amy Klco

I am the story-seer.
I see the world,
I see the people,
I see their stories,
but no one sees me.

In ancient times,
those who knew the stories
were revered,
treated special because
of what they could do,
of what they could see.
I know the stories,
I see them every day
but I can't tell them
because no one see me,
no one hears me.
My voice is silent
to them.

I walk through the halls
of my high school,
seeing all
and being seen by none.
Sometimes I wonder if I really
am invisible—like it's
a superpower.
But I know I'm not.
When I walk through the halls
kids move around me.
In class, my teacher
marks me present.
But nobody really sees.
The blessing—
the curse—
of being the quiet kid.
I see her pain—the

one that you call "fat,"
the one you judge
on how she looks
without ever knowing
who she is inside.
I see her silent cries,
the tears she never
dares to shed.
I see his pain—the
one that you call "fag,"
because he's different,
because he's gentle,
because he's softer than you.
You try to make him hard,
make him give up
all that he has to share,
to make him more like you—
to make him safe from you.

And I see you
trying so hard to fit in
to be "cool," to be
accepted,
to be what others
want you to be,
to never be yourself.

And I realize they are
the lucky ones—the ones
you call "fat" and "gay,"
and "slut," and "nerd"
and "weirdo."
They, at least, are real.
You label them,
but they know
who they are.
And you have no idea.

❀ ❀ ❀

You put on your mask
every morning
and fight to fit in.
And you think no one
sees your real story.
But I see....

I can't be seen,
But oh, how I see.
And oh, all the stories.
I could tell....

Amy Klco wrote her first book at the age of ten and has been writing ever since. Klco has BAs in English and Art, and MAs in Education, Literacy, and Special Education. She's taught secondary school for 13 years and has experienced bullying first-hand. The poem "The Story-Seer" is the inspiration for her novella, *YANA: You Are Not Alone.* Learn more about her work at enchantment-press.com or on Facebook at https://www.facebook.com/amyjkklco.

WW I marchiing band, Sault Ste. Marie

Lonely Road

by Becky Ross Michael

"It probably won't snow much," he assured me. His voice was confident, but concern flashed in his eyes behind wire-rimmed glasses. Was that worry connected to the driving conditions or to the direction we were taking in our relationship? I sat down on a bench outside the mom-and-pop restaurant in Munising and quickly exchanged shoes for fur-lined boots. Since we had no good way to communicate on the road, we agreed ahead of time to meet there for lunch. The waitress had alerted us to some messy weather on our intended route along the lakeshore, at the same time she offered dessert of apple or raspberry pie.

I was moving from downstate Michigan to join him in the Upper Peninsula city of Marquette, where we planned to give our marriage another try. He waited for a large logging truck to pass, waved a little salute, and then carefully pulled his dark Jeep and the trailer that carried my belongings onto the road. I followed in my small, silver car and watched the first flurries of the season begin to decorate the landscape.

While I drove, I focused on our future together and hoped we had made a good decision. Typically a nervous winter motorist, I tried to push away any anxiety about slippery roads. Fewer vehicles shared the two-lane highway with each mile, and the area became increasingly remote. Pine and bare hardwood trees were thick, and homes or businesses became scarce. The few towns and villages we passed were each marked by a lone stoplight or blinker.

The flakes fell faster, blown by escalating winds. For better concentration, I turned Van Morrison down a bit and switched my fan onto high for more heat. Rarely catching sight of the Jeep through the thickening white, I reduced my speed to keep the car from sliding.

When I passed the first snowplow, I was relieved the county was prepared for the early blizzard. Even so, they seemed to be having trouble staying ahead of the swiftly falling snow. I fought the wheel to hold my course and regretted that my vehicle was so light.

Weather near Lake Superior is famously extreme and can change drastically without warning. A perky voice on the radio suggested that Marquette would receive only a dusting, and I expected to be out of the worst of it before long. Although the clock read early afternoon, the sky was a deep leaden-gray. A pickup with darkened headlights passed me, and I flashed mine, hoping they got the message. I stared ahead and followed imprints of tires that shifted with each gust. Time slowed to a crawl.

The Jeep must have been well ahead of me, since I hadn't seen it in quite a while. My fingers gripped the steering wheel too tightly, going numb, and I tried to relax them. I shifted my body forward in an attempt to see the road more clearly through the effects of the howling wind.

Any expectation of heat for my toes long abandoned, I diverted all warm air toward the defroster to retain a clear view. My wipers laboriously worked to clear the expanse of glass, but to no avail. Ice began to form on the blades, and portions of my windshield became opaque.

I followed what seemed to be a single vehicle track, at times, and avoided the disappearing ditches. I wondered occasionally if

I was even on the right side of the road in that tunnel of white. Minutes felt like hours. Although my teeth chattered from the cold, I detected droplets of sweat trickling between my breasts. Heart pounding in my ears, I knew that pulling off the road was a magnet for trouble, but finally felt there was no choice.

In the stilled car, I turned on my emergency flashers and wondered how he fared. His Jeep with four-wheel drive was more suited for the weather, but hauled that unfamiliar trailer. Through the span of thick whiteness, I saw a barely visible, blinking light moving toward me. Another plow, I guessed, and prayed that its driver could see my vehicle where it sat. In relief, I determined it was well on the opposite side, as it crawled closer. When it stopped across from my snow-covered car, the driver cranked down his window and motioned for me to do the same.

"Broken down, ma'am?" the ruddy-faced man hollered.

"No. I can't see where I'm going," I called back.

"Good," I was surprised to hear him respond, over the sounds of the gale. "There's a place back a bit, from the way you came. A parking lot to get off the road."

"Didn't see it," I responded, shaking my head in the negative.

"Turn around, and I'll lead you there," he yelled and rolled the glass closed before I could answer.

My whole body vibrated from cold and fear. I searched both ways through the whiteout for any oncoming traffic and held my breath. The car struggled for traction and finally completed a slow u-turn, while I joined the giant machine in a wintry parade. After a mile or two, the driver reached his arm out the window and pointed a gloved hand to the left. I spied a parking lot that held several cars covered in white, tooted my horn in thanks, and turned.

Through deep drifts exposing few traces of recent activity, I drove close to the building. After my engine was quieted, I first heard a loud ringing in my ears, followed by silence only the insulation of thick snow and ice can provide. I grabbed my hat and gloves from the seat and started the short trek up to what the dilapidated, crooked sign announced as the "Tioga Tavern."

At a small table near the dancing fire, I took off my gloves and held a cup of coffee for comfort, more than anything else. I assured the welcoming bartender that I wasn't interested in something to eat. His eyes seemed curious about my situation, but he didn't ask. Peanut shells embellished the floor, and a silent, old-fashioned jukebox rested on the other side of the scarred, wooden dance floor. It must have been quite the hot spot on a Saturday night.

Not sure what to do next, I waited for the adrenaline to subside and willed the weather to clear. I hated making him worry, but knew he might be driving on toward Marquette without even realizing my absence. I also feared he may have slid off the road and needed help. If I called the police, would they look for someone missing in the storm?

Besides the bartender, the only inhabitants that stormy afternoon were a few ancient men in flannel shirts and suspenders, who played some sort of a card game at a table, and several talkative couples at the bar. While I sipped the hot, bitter liquid and argued with my inner self over what action to take, I heard a jingle from the door. A burst of cold air followed a laughing, young couple into the room. They climbed onto stools at the bar and ordered hot chocolates fortified by peppermint schnapps. After they took turns visiting the restroom, they settled in to sample their drinks.

"Man, it's nasty out," the young man said to the bartender. "Would you believe, we passed a crazy guy walkin', back there! He was tryin' to find a woman's car. Said she might've gone in the ditch, and he needed to walk so he wouldn't miss her."

"I wonder..." started the man behind the bar, glancing my direction.

Jolted by their words, I took a deep breath and joined them. "Excuse me, but I couldn't help but overhear. Can you tell me what the man looked like?" I asked the newcomers.

St. Ignace and Mackinaw Island

"Hard to tell under all that winter gear, but he seemed to have a reddish beard," the young man answered.

"He wore glasses," his female companion said. "They were kinda frosting over."

I grabbed my gloves, headed to the door, and opened to the wailing blizzard. Like frozen sand, it stung my eyes and I raised my hands to protect them. Peering beyond the expanse of the parking lot, I saw a hooded figure in a heavy winter coat adorned by patches of white. He trudged alongside the road with his head bent against the icy onslaught.

Wild laughter of reprieve bubbled up from inside, and I yelled against the wind. I ran toward him through peaks and valleys of snow, like in a dream where movement is almost impossible. Since he didn't see or hear me, his head remained down as he plodded determinedly ahead. When he finally sensed movement, his head jerked up to meet my familiar face. He veered off what was probably the shoulder of the road and headed toward me. Finally close enough, I leapt at him, and he caught me in his arms.

"Are you okay?" he asked, in a voice nearly stolen by the wind.

"Now I am," I answered, so sure that our life would be good.

I solemnly looked toward his eyes. He gazed back, removed his mitten, and tenderly touched my cheek.

In our many years together that followed, we often traveled that same isolated stretch of highway. The sign for the Tioga Tavern still hung lopsidedly from the front of the building. No matter the season, the windows remained dark, and no visitors were seen approaching its door. Had that warm building and the helpful people within been real, or were they figments of my imagination? I may never again feel the complete certainty about anything as I did on that day.

Originally from Lower Michigan, **Becky Ross Michael** worked as an educator in Calumet and Sault Ste. Marie. Her fiction has been published in *Ellery Queen Mystery Magazine*, and her writing for kids appears in a web-enabled program for at-risk students. To be closer to her daughters and their families, she moved to a pleasant location in Texas, where she will always long for the beauty that is Michigan. Find out more about her at https://platformnumber4.wordpress.com.

An Abandoned Dream

by Elizabeth Fust

What becomes of imaginary friends who are forgotten? We become but unattached shadows. We follow constantly along, not like shadows of reality which disappear with weather and changes of setting. Not imaginary, but no longer imagined. We slink and traipse along the streets, silhouettes of unfulfilled hopes and dreams. Here an astronaut. Here a magician. And here I am, a ballerina.

Like these hopes and dreams, we are forgotten, abandoned, unseen to all save the occasional spotting by those we might call charge or friend. Only then we are construed as nightmares or monsters. What if we could be brought back from memories' depths of oblivion, where perhaps we slipped into or were forced? What if this non-substance shade could again wear color and recount former adventures, which before had never been made alone? So I shall tell you of our plight. Just I, a little ballerina.

She was very young when she abandoned me. *This is no world for ballerinas*, she was told. Or, *you will never be good enough to be successful.* So I became to her an anchor rather than kite. Thus I was cut loose. From that time I followed her, turning pirouettes and leaping, but unable to hold again her mind. Ignored. Blocked out, shadow though I am, to make way for duller matters than I.

Some days she might see me. Though not as I am or to her I once was. My sugar plum tiara turned into a monster's horn. My crinoline tutu become the body of a misshaped creature. My satin pointe shoes twisted into spikes of deadly affliction. Having forced or willingly overlaid this visage upon me, over what I truly am, she rushes past to avoid me—a dangerous dream become a nightmare.

Pirouetting around the backyard. Leaping over cracks in the sidewalk. Curtsying to anyone who might applaud. Once we did these together, now I do alone. Never to weary in my dance, though lonely sadness is my music. Cursed and locked in this colorless two-dimensional realm of shadow forever more.

Then one night, one night after decades, we went to the theater. She dressed in rosy pink taffeta, satin shoes, hair in a bun. I don't think she recognized the significance of her costume. I stepped slowly through the shadows of the crowd, around pillars and under arches. Yet under the light of the chandelier as she slowly spun in wonder, she saw me. Not a shadow, but a ballerina, my true self. Then she turned away.

Yet there was hope! Sweet hope! Though she sat in a balcony and I stood on the stage far off, as the music grew, the lights dimmed, her eyes alighted on me and I began to glow once more. In an instant, color rushed me, tiara sparkled, tutu no longer tattered shadow rags.

As the corps of *Giselle* were raised on pointe so I was, too, and began to dance! Giselle, a girl in love and full of life and dance. With every note, I soared across the stage higher than any prima ballerina. I spun faster and longer. I was more bird than ballerina. As her smile grew so did mine.

Through intermission she saw me still, even in the powder room mirror behind her as she fixed her bun. I was beside her, with her. I was alive once more. Dreams lived. Through the second act we were magnificent. Even as

Wholeback steamship - 1890s

Giselle passed on to become a ghost, a Wilis, a cursed phantom to her living love; even as a corps of Wilis passed across the stage, arms held to carry unfulfilled dreams; even as Giselle's lover escaped a dancing death back to the light of day, *Giselle* was made our own. With the final note, final bow, the applause, the smiles, I became transcendent. More than shadow, color, or glowing. So real, I was almost reality.

As I stood on stage staring up at her and she with affection returned these looks, a companion turned to her and said, "So young, this fleeting beauty. What kind of life is this? What success and fulfillment can come from prancing across the stage, playacting silly stories? Come, let's go back to real life. Perhaps someday to come again, but such false things taint the hard working mind."

The companion left and it was she alone on balcony and I alone on stage. She looked down on me. Her eyes dimmed. So did I. Past shadows to nothing I diminished as she turned away and made me no dream, no shadow, no nightmare, no more.

As I was nothing, I stayed there. Halted in time and space, in a nothing realm of forgotten day dreams.

Until came a stage hand with a lighted bulb on a pole. He came and said, "Here,

ghosts, your light. Be you not lost, though forgotten. So you may see your way, though you be unseen. Here, ghosts, a feeble light for home."

There upon this single light I was made new. Not shadow, though not painted. I was dim, foggy, lacking focus of a mind, but yet given substance in this actors' theater more than I had been given in the world outside. Around me here I saw a knight, here a doctor, here a novelist. And here I am, a ballerina. For this audience of ghosts I did dance. For these theatergoers were forgotten hopes and dreams left in this home to all. In this house-made-home we do visit where reality and fiction blur, with what is real and not. Perhaps to someday once again inspire an imagination.

Elizabeth Fust is currently studying Writing and Communication Studies at Northern Michigan University. She is a senior editor and the web editor for NMU's undergraduate run online literary journal *The Ore Ink Review*. She is also a member of Sigma Tau Delta International English Honor Society and has presented a short story at the Sigma Tau Delta 2016 International Convention.

Jacqui, Marilyn, & Shelly

by Terry Sanders

Mike had been thinking all morning about how many of his coworkers were not only chauvinistic but down right misogynists. Today's coffee break conversation had been filled with disparaging comments about their wives and girlfriends. This close to Christmas, he thought they would have been more complimentary. Looking around, he noticed that everyone was gone in his work group except Shelly, the Admin Aid. Perhaps the rest were shopping during lunch for presents for those they had earlier criticized.

On Shelly's desk, a bouquet of roses gave Mike an opportunity to ask her discretely if she had been embarrassed when he fixed the jammed zipper of her high topped boot while she was wearing it three days ago. When he asked, she first surveyed the room to see if they were alone.

"No," she answered.

Her abrupt response prompted him to try a different tack. "What's the occasion for the flowers?"

"My boyfriend gave them to me for my birthday, but don't tell anybody."

"That was nice of him...and a bold gesture too." Mike added with deference to her reputed shyness, trying to get to the question he was most intent to ask. But she interpreted his last comment to be directed at her boyfriend.

"It might have been stronger if he had delivered them himself today instead of having them sent. Can you believe he was the one who convinced me to go through assertiveness training?"

"So today is your birthday?"

"Yes."

"Let me take you to lunch to celebrate," he offered, thinking a change of scenery might calm the mood that seemed to be developing.

"I'd like to if we could stop at the maintenance garage on the way. That way I could get the end-of-year mileage on a car that's in for repair. It would save me a trip over there alone."

•••

The restaurant they chose was only ten minutes away. On the walk and while waiting for their order, they talked about each of their family's birthday rituals. The holiday mood of the other patrons combined with their own discussion, raised both of their spirits.

When they arrived at the Federal motor pool garage, they proceeded down the ramps to level five. Part of Shelly's job was to be the branch property book officer so she had the key for the vehicle key lock box. As she opened it, Mike noticed a key tag that piqued his interest.

"What is the one marked 'LIMO' for?"

"For that big black thing over in the corner."

She was pointing at a stretch limousine in the darkest corner of the level they were on. While Shelly got the mileage, Mike went to look at the limo. It was an early fifties model Cadillac. He was still staring at it when she came over to him.

"This one is almost like the one I borrowed for my high school prom. Could we get the key for it so I might look at the inside?"

"I don't know... well maybe if we're quick about it."

•••

As they were sitting in the back seat admiring the luxury, Shelly asked, "How did you get to borrow something like this?"

"My boss owned a hotel and he had one to chauffer people back and forth to the airport and for wedding party guests."

"This one is used to get people from the airport too... mostly politicians but sometimes foreign dignitaries. One time when I first started working here, they used it to pick up President Carter, but he didn't stop at our building."

"I'll bet the driver has some good stories to tell," Mike thought to himself.

Just then they heard voices getting louder and closer from the next level up. When the first of the two men was far enough down the ramp to see his entire height, Mike said to Shelly, "Duck down!" She turned and lay on her back on the seat giving him nowhere to go but half on top of her.

The first mechanic said to the other, "I don't see it here. It must've been returned already." When the sounds of retreating footsteps had stopped, Mike looked through the window to make sure they were gone. He looked down while claiming the coast was clear and was met with a strange smile from Shelly. Her look was explained by a question.

"Is this where I get my birthday kiss?"

"Sure," he said, trying not to show any surprise at her initiative.

Mike had to shift his weight more on top of her to have their mouths line up enough for a modest and discrete kiss. This forced him to be precariously balanced with both hands on the seat.

Just as he slowly started to put his lips close to hers, his right hand slipped into the crease between the bench and the back of the seat causing him to fall about three inches tightly upon her. Shelly's only reaction was to broaden her smile.

"What the..." Mike moaned feeling some metallic object pressing into the side of his hand supporting half his weight. "Are you ok? I'm not usually this clumsy."

"Clumsy? I thought it was enthusiasm. You can try it again if you think you can be more graceful."

•••

On the way back to the office, Mike was rolling over in his mind the possible reasons for Shelly's private display of affection for him. His best guess was the occasion a few days prior when he helped her remove a jam in the zipper of her boot. The remedy involved Mike sticking his hand inside the boot along her thigh to pull the fleece lining out of the zipper. Her facial expression on that day was more painful than the one he had seen just a few minutes ago.

A second mystery Mike was trying to solve was the object that cut the side of his hand when it slipped into the crease of the limo seat. He had retrieved it and it was in his pocket and just now returning to the front of his thoughts. It looked like a bushing or a ring of sorts made from a familiar kind of key stock. He knew he had seen it somewhere before but could not remember where.

By the time they arrived back at work, it dawned on him where he had seen it. He got off the elevator on the fourth floor. leaving Shelly to continue to the tenth where they worked. Mike was almost sure the ring was made from a munitions' locker key. He had met a member of the Coast Guard administrative group on the fourth floor who had been a CPO in the Navy. Mike hoped the Chief could verify his hunch. He did not correctly explain where he found it.

"Yah, that's a detonator safe key. Or it was," the Chief said.

The centering tab at the end of the shank along with the rest of the key was wrapped into a circle and hooked into the keyring hole in the twist plate.

"If it wasn't so corroded, I could find out what kind of a boat it came from," the chief added. "It's probably not afloat anymore though. That's the kind of souvenir a skipper would keep of a vessel that sank under his command. I'll bet it was from a small surface craft, or maybe a sub."

Mike thanked him for his opinion and got a small amount of Brasso with a promise to clean it up and let the Chief know if there was any identifying number on it.

•••

Returning to his work area, Mike walked past a discussion between two of the most prurient of his coworkers. They were speculating on causes for the scratches on Shelly's cheek. She was not at her desk at the moment, but he had stopped in the bathroom to try the brass polish on the ring making his arrival fifteen or so minutes later than hers. After listening to a couple of illogical and unkind circumstances that could have been a cause, Mike offered a suggestion that was actually true with only one detail changed.

"If you dorks hadn't skated out early for lunch, you might've seen her give a passionate kiss to her boyfriend when he delivered those flowers on her desk."

The ploy worked. They both accepted Mike's proposed cause and got back to work, failing to notice that he had not shaved in two days. All that was left was to intercept Shelly to corroborate the yarn he had just spun.

He turned in his chair so that he could see the office door and Shelly's desk at the same time. While he waited, he continued to polish the ring. Within minutes and before she returned, the stamped letters and numbers showed clear enough to read, *PT-109*.

Terry Sanders, currently living in Manistique, MI since retirement in 2006, worked as a mechanical designer, environmental technician and contractor preparing operation and assembly manuals. She received a BA from Univ. of WI. Among her publications are: High school textbook for Mythology, short works of fiction presented to workshops at the Second Saturday writers group in Curtis (MI), and currently a modern novella version of *The Iliad*.

Shipwreck - woodcut by Moran

Marquette Medium

by Tyler Tichelaar

"Is this Sybil Shelley?" asked the woman on the other end of the phone.

"Yes," I said.

"Are you the ghost hunter?"

"Well, I'm a medium. I try to help ghosts and people."

"I saw your Facebook page. My name is Julie, and I need your help."

I had just moved back to Marquette a few weeks ago. I was looking for a job, but I didn't want to experience the nine-to-five grind, so I decided to advertise my medium skills online to see whether anyone would hire me.

I had left Marquette twelve years ago, believing it was time to spread my wings, but I'd always known someday I would return, and now my intuition had told me it was the right time.

"I'd be happy to help you," I told Julie. "What's the situation?"

"My father just moved into that old orphanage building—the one they recently fixed up and turned into apartments. He's only been there for a month, but some weird things have been happening."

"Weird like how?"

"Well, he'll set something down, but when he comes back, it's not there."

"Oh," I said. "Can I ask how old your father is?"

"He's seventy-eight, but it's not like he has dementia or anything."

"Have there been any other strange happenings?"

"Yes," said Julie. "I actually experienced this when I visited him last night...."

She hesitated until I said, "Go ahead; it's okay."

"Well, there aren't any children in the building, but he can hear a little girl crying. I heard it too—it seemed to be coming from his bedroom closet, but when we opened the door, no one was there."

"That does sound like a ghost."

"Can you help us?"

"I'll try."

I explained to her what I actually did and my fees. She agreed to all of that, so I asked for her father's apartment number and said I'd meet her there at 7 p.m.

•••

When I knocked on the apartment door, a middle-aged woman opened it.

"You must be Julie," I said.

"Yes, and you're Sybil. It's a pleasure to meet you."

As I stepped into the apartment, I saw Julie's father, whom she introduced as Rodger, standing by the bedroom door.

"She's in here," he said, immediately ushering me into his room.

I stepped into the bedroom and looked around.

"Do you sense her?" asked Julie.

"I'm not sure," I said.

"She's in here," Rodger said. And before I could stop him, he opened the closet door.

"If you don't mind," I said, "I'd like to be left alone. We might all scare her off, and I need to concentrate to see whether I can sense anything."

I looked at Rodger as I spoke, but he didn't reply. He turned, looked at Julie, and frowned.

"I think it should be okay, Dad," she said.

She put her hand on his shoulder and guided him out the door. "We'll be in the living room," she told me. "Take as long as you need. Will it disturb you if we watch TV?"

"No, that's fine," I said.

They left the room, Julie shutting the door behind them. I was reluctant to sit down on the unmade bed, so I opted for the floor in front of the closet. By then, I could hear Vanna White's letters lighting up for her to turn—I hadn't counted on Rodger being half-deaf.

I sat there for a while. Only when it started to get dark did I sense anything—a change in room temperature. Suddenly, the bedroom light flickered on and off several times.

"I'm scared of the dark." It was a little girl, and she was whispering in my ear.

"I am too," I replied.

"The nuns won't let us have a light on."

"They should," I said to empathize with her.

She didn't say anything more, but I could sense movement, as if she were walking around me. Then I heard the voice again, but this time it came from inside the closet.

"You're pretty."

"Thank you," I replied. "So are you."

I couldn't see her as an apparition, but I was getting an image of her in my mind—a little girl, maybe eight or nine, but a bit small for her age. She had long hair tied back in a ponytail and a plain blue dress, almost like a school uniform.

"What's your name?" I asked.

Suddenly, she turned shy. I could envision her looking down at her feet.

"Sister says not to talk to strangers."

"It's okay," I said. "I'm a friend. What's your sister's name?"

"Not my sister!" she laughed. "Sister Euphrasia."

"Oh, one of the nuns?" I asked.

"Yes."

"Do you have any sisters of your own?"

"No-o.... Well, except for Lyla."

"Who?" I asked because the name startled me. I had known a Lyla when I lived in Marquette before—she had been raised in the orphanage—but she was probably dead by now. She'd have to be about ninety.

"Lyla. She's my best friend, but she's more like a sister because she looks out for me."

"I see," I said. "Is your name Bel?"

"Sister doesn't like me being called that. She says my name is Belinda. I only let Lyla call me Bel."

She was the woman I thought—Lyla's best friend. The two had lived at Snowberry Heights—the senior citizen high-rise—when I had known them, but I hadn't known that Bel had died.

"Is Lyla here with you?" I asked.

"No. I don't know where she is. I keep looking for her. Everyone is strange here. I don't know who that man is. Is he the new janitor? Where have all the children gone?"

"I don't think they're here anymore, Bel. They all went away a long time ago."

"Why?"

"They grew up."

"Uh uh," she insisted. "They couldn't grow up that fast. I'm not growed up."

"Bel, don't you remember being grown up?"

"Uh uh," she said. "I can't be growed up. I'm just a little girl."

"But Lyla is grown up," I said. "Don't you remember? You both lived at Snowberry Heights the last time I saw you."

"I never saw you before."

"You did. At Snowberry—you were both senior citizens living there."

"What's a seenyor sitzen?"

"Someone who is old. Bel, you and Lyla were old ladies together. Honey, you must have died. You're a spirit now."

"You're crazy, lady!" she shouted.

"No, honey, I—"

"Lyla will know. She'll know you're crazy. I'll tell her so...only I don't know where she is."

"Oh, honey," I said, and I reached out as if to hug her, but then my image of her vanished.

I waited a few minutes. When she didn't come back, I got up and opened the bedroom door.

Julie heard me and got up off the couch. She poked her dad, who was asleep in his chair.

"Well?" he said, turning to stare at me.

"I know who she is," I said. "I mean, I did. I actually knew her before she passed away."

"Whose kid is she?" asked Julie.

"It's not like that," I said. "She—when I knew her, she was in her seventies, but for some reason, she thinks she's a little girl again. She's very confused."

"Can you get rid of her?" asked Rodger.

"I... I think so, but I need help from someone."

"Who?" asked Julie.

"That's the thing. I don't know whether the person I need help from is even still alive. It's the woman who was her best friend. I'll try to find her tomorrow."

"What about tonight?" asked Rodger. "I can't sleep with no little girl crying in my closet."

"Dad," said Julie, "you can wait one more night, can't you?"

He frowned, but he finally grumbled, "I guess I'll have to. My back is too bad for sleeping on the couch."

•••

In the morning, I looked in the phone book—if Lyla were still alive, I suspected she'd still have a landline. Sure enough, there she was. "She's still alive," I thought, "but will she remember me?"

I dialed the number and waited for her to answer.

"Hello."

"Is this Lyla?" I asked.

"Who wants to know?"

It was definitely her.

"Lyla," I said, "I don't know if you remember me, but this is Sybil Shelley—we used to go to the Women on Wednesdays group."

"Sybil? Of course I remember you. Are you back in Marquette?"

"Yes, I just moved back, and I thought I'd call to see how you were. I'm sorry we lost touch. I was never good about sending Christmas cards."

"Neither am I."

"Are you busy?" I asked. "I was wondering whether I could come over to visit."

"Sure. I just had my coffee, but I'll make some more."

I told her I'd see her in twenty minutes. After all, you don't tell someone her best friend is a ghost over the phone.

•••

"You've gotta be shitting me!" Lyla exclaimed after I explained the situation to her. She might have been surprised, but she was no frail old lady subject to shock. She'd always been on the tough side—I imagine being raised in an orphanage can do that to you.

I reassured her I was telling the truth.

"If anyone else told me this," she said, and then she put her elbows on the kitchen table and buried her face in her hands. After a moment, she removed her hands and said, "It was so hard, Sybil. Bel had dementia. I moved her in here with me. She slept in my bed and I slept on the couch. Other than having someone come to bathe her, I did everything for her—for three years. Then one day, she wouldn't get out of bed. I called the ambulance and they took her to the hospital. She died two days later—pneumonia. I was so afraid she'd have to go to a nursing home, but...."

I reached across the table and took her hand.

"I'm sorry, Lyla. I know you loved her. It must have been very hard."

"It's okay," she said, grabbing a Kleenex. "You do what you have to do."

After she wiped her eyes, I said, "You certainly did a lot for her, Lyla, but she needs your help again."

"What do you mean?"

"I think her dementia left her confused or maybe she was just happiest as a child, but either way, she needs to go into the light."

"The light?" She looked puzzled.

"Yes. It's like heaven. You've heard stories, I'm sure, of people who have near-death experiences and see a light or a tunnel and someone coming for them. Bel's an earth-bound spirit right now—she doesn't realize that she's dead. She needs you to tell her it's okay to go into the light—to go to heaven."

"I don't know," said Lyla. "Shouldn't the priest do that?"

"No," I said. "You're the only one Bel really trusts. You need to tell her. She'll listen to you."

"It's just crazy," she said.

"So is most of life. Will you do it, for Bel's sake?"

•••

At seven-thirty that evening, Lyla and I were standing in front of Rodger's apartment door.

"This is crazy," Lyla repeated. "If anyone other than you told me this, Sybil, I'd think they'd lost their mind."

Julie let us inside. Rodger was in his chair. Vanna was already turning her letters.

"It's nice to meet you," said Julie, shaking Lyla's hand. "So Sybil tells me you grew up here in the orphanage."

"Yeah," Lyla said, "but it sure wasn't nice like this when I lived here."

"Will it be all right if we just sit in the bedroom again?" I asked.

Julie nodded, showed us to the bedroom, and told us to let her know if we needed anything. Then she shut the door.

"What a mess," muttered Lyla, looking around. She pulled up the crumpled bedspread so she could sit on the end of the bed.

"Let's just sit here quietly," I said. "After a few minutes, hopefully Bel will come."

I closed my eyes. I could feel Lyla staring at me, unsure whether I was meditating or sleeping. I could sense how uncomfortable she was. I didn't blame her.

Suddenly, I felt a jolt to the back of my head—as if Bel were inside me.

"You found her!" Bel shrieked joyfully.

"I did," I said out loud.

"You did what?" asked Lyla.

"Bel is here," I explained.

"Where? I don't see nothing."

"She's—well, she's on the bed, behind us."

By now, I had opened my eyes. I put my arm around Lyla's shoulders so she wouldn't turn around, see nothing, and not believe me.

"How do I know she's there if I don't look?" asked Lyla.

"Just trust me," I said. "Please. Let me talk to her for a minute."

"Ow!" said Lyla.

"What's wrong?"

"She pulled my hair. She used to do that all the time when we were kids."

For a minute, Lyla looked pissed, but then she suddenly laughed.

"Bel," she said. "I miss you."

"I miss you too," said Bel.

"She says she misses you," I told Lyla.

"Is she okay?"

"She says...you look really old."

"I'll be ninety next year. It won't be long before I join you, Bel."

"She doesn't understand. Explain to her... that she's—"

"Bel," said Lyla, "I hate to tell you this, but you're dead." Then she laughed. "You need to... come out of the closet... and... well, go to heaven."

"She's asking you how."

"I don't know how," Lyla told me.

"Yes, you do," I said. "Remember—the light."

"Oh, yeah. Bel, there's this light. Can you see a light?"

"She says no."

"Bel, you have to go to Heaven. You know, to be with Jesus, like the nuns taught us."

"She says she's afraid. She's afraid she'll be alone there."

"You won't be, Bel," Lyla assured her. "Bel, your parents will be there."

I waited. No message was coming through. Had we lost her? Then I heard:

"I see a light."

"She sees the light," I told Lyla.

"Go to the light, Bel," Lyla said. "Please. It'll be okay."

"She says she loves you, Lyla. She wishes you were going with her."

"Bel, I'll come soon. I promise. I love you too."

"She says...." But then I broke off. I couldn't help it. I started crying too. I was just so happy because of what Bel was saying after she'd waited so long.

"What?" asked Lyla.

"She says her parents are there."

Lyla started crying now. "Go be with your family, Bel."

"Her parents have their arms around her. They're walking into the light.... She's crossed over."

Lyla turned to look at me, and through tears, she said, "She's not an orphan anymore."

Then we hold each other for a little while until Pat Sajak gives the wheel a final spin.

Tyler R. Tichelaar is the author of *The Marquette Trilogy, Spirit of the North: a Paranormal Romance, The Best Place, The Gothic Wanderer*, and numerous other books. His next book, *Haunted Marquette*, will be released in October 2017. Find out more about Tyler and his books at www.MarquetteFiction.com.

U.P. Reader is accepting submissions for Issue #2

The Upper Peninsula Publishers and Authors Association (UPPAA) presents a new publication called the *U.P. Reader*. This will be an annual anthology that will feature the collected works of the best of the authors of the Upper Peninsula.

"The *U.P. Reader* is something I hope will put Upper Peninsula authors in touch with the readers to expand their exposure to a much greater and more effective level," commented Committee Chair, Mikel B. Classen.

This collection will be published by the UPPAA and will showcase the multitude of talent within the membership of the organization. The *U.P. Reader* will average 45 – 50K words and will include all genres of writing including short stories, non-fiction and poetry. Artwork and photography pertaining to submissions are encouraged.

The *U.P. Reader* will be available to booksellers as well as authors for sale and promotion. This will allow the members an opportunity to participate in a project that will not only showcase their talents as writers but also to get the finished product in front of readers so they can discover the U.P. authors that interest them no matter what their reading preference.

Submissions will be juried by a panel and those chosen will appear in the *U.P. Reader*. Authors chosen to be published in the anthology will see their submission published along with an author's bio to steer readers to more work by that author.

"This is a publication about discovery. Finding new favorites and maybe rediscovering some old ones too. I think it is underestimated how many really talented writers we have living right here in the U.P. and the Reader will be the place to find them." said Mikel Classen.

Tyler Tichelaar, President of UPPAA, adds, "A collection of short stories, poetry, and essays will allow readers to enjoy a hodgepodge of U.P. literature from many different voices and will offer numerous visions and definitions of what it means to live here. The U.P. can be many different things to many different people and such a collection will help make that clear."

Proceeds from the U.P. Reader will be used to support operating costs of the UPPAA and its many events to educate its members about writing and publishing and to get U.P. literature into the hands of potential readers.

The deadline for submitting for the next issue of U.P. Reader will be November 15th, 2017.

"I'm really excited about what we've received so far," said Mikel Classen, project head for the U.P. Reader. "I really want to see more."

For more information, including submission guidelines, contact:

editor@UPReader.org

or visit us online at http://upreader.org/submission-guidelines/

The House on Blakely Hill

by Mikel B. Classen

It is said that Satan himself led Elias Blakely to the spot on which he built his home of horror. That wasn't quite true. What led Blakely to the ancient cave was much older than that. It was a thing of chaos, born of the earth when its appearance was still undecided. It had been cast out as having no place in a world of order. It had found a friend in Elias Blakely.

The place was atop a high hill. The cave mouth led down at a steep angle, but it was walkable. Within moments it opened into a large cavern. The floor was flat rock, granite smooth. Before him, Elias saw a great stone that by all appearances looked as if it were an altar. But how could that be? It motioned toward the stone. A voice surrounded Elias, seeming to come from everywhere. The formless thing made something that resembled an arm and pointed. "It is from here that you call me." Elias saw glyphs and symbols decorating the altar and the surrounding walls. There had been men here at some long lost time. The worn rock told of activity from long past. Or were they men? Maybe they were something else.

Blakely waited anxiously for the demand he knew would come. They made a pact, struck a bargain. It spoke again, "You must always remain here or the pact will be broken. My anger will be visited upon all Blakelys for generations."

"The pact will be honored," Elias pledged. His voice echoed through the chamber. He took out a blade and made a cut across his forearm. Blood dripped into the swirling mass that was the hand of the thing. A long "Ahhhhh" escaped from it, a distinct sigh in the cavern.

"The doorway is open. The pact is made. It is as agreed, no Blakely shall ever want. Secrets of chaos shall be yours."

It was on that ground that Blakely constructed a great mansion, a Victorian castle made of granite and marble. No expense was spared and craftsmen from across the world were brought to create a home of beauty and curiosity. After its construction, the Blakelys shut themselves off from the rest of the world. This spawned a continuous flow of gossip.

It is said that Blakely willingly allowed his wife, Sarah, to be bred with a demon. It is said she died giving birth to the hell-spawn child as it clawed its way out of the womb. It is said Elizabeth Alice, the child, was locked away in an asylum with madness until her death. A sound described only as chittering and chattering was heard by attendants as black "angels" came to claim her spirit as she died, so it is said.

The elder Blakely remarried and his second wife gave birth to a son. She too died after flinging herself from a second story window to the cobblestones below. Her skull cracked open upon impact. She was buried next to Sarah in the family plot without ceremony.

The son, Israel, was rarely seen. His father preferred to have the boy tutored at home with a special curriculum that he alone approved. Since no one local would venture near the Blakely Mansion, a governess was sent for, a black woman from Jamaica, named Angeline.

Few knew what went on behind the closed doors on Blakely Hill, but many were willing to speculate. The stories of black magic and sacrificial rituals with devils and demons ran rampant, but the few locals that perpetuated the stories over beer and booze never were able to muster the courage to do anything beyond gossip.

It was when Angeline came to town that it all began to change. She'd come to run an errand. She'd attempted to be secretive—a wrong turn and Angeline was exposed. She was seen. It was the necklace she wore and strange dress that frightened them. Her dark black skin inspired irrational fear. On a pendant there was the figure of a man and what appeared to be a small human skull as a head, a small bird skull with the beak removed. They were common in her homeland. In the quiet isolated village, it was all terrifying.

The small group of villagers that surrounded her began to press in closer. She knew the threat; she'd seen it before. She waved her hand in front of her and her eyes got big. She began to speak in a language unknown to them. They backed away; some left. She moved and gyrated into strange contortions and shook her necklace with the skull at those that were left. They scurried away in fear. She returned to the mansion.

"She's a witch. They're practicing witchcraft up at the Blakely house," one drunken farmer at the tavern started. "I'd always suspected as much. Yes I did. I been tellin' ya all along."

"What good is it?" said another.

"If we don't do something, they're going to curse us all or sacrifice us to some evil. Right they are. The evil that starts at that house is gonna spread and keep spreading until it infects us all. We gotta do something about it, I say."

"We can't just kill them," commented another.

"They're in league with Satan, the place should be burned. There are demons up there. Old Elias calls them up. Next his son

will be doing the same thing. Our village will never escape the evil they do."

"He's right," yelled the tavern owner from behind his bar. Strangely, courage was found hiding in the room. It began in murmurs and then rose to enthusiasm accompanied by glasses of ale.

"If we end the family line, their black evil will be done."

It was late in the night before they left the tavern. The group of men marched to Blakely Hill, with alcohol-fortified determination in their steps. It had been decided that the place should be burned with all inside. They'd tried them, and found them guilty of crimes against men and God. Even the child.

Elias Blakely knew of their coming. A voice whispered it in his ear as he slept. He awoke angry. In his mind he saw them coming, drunken sots bent on destroying his family, his work. Angeline and Israel accompanied him through the hidden stair that led to the chamber below. It was a subterranean cavern that was vast.

Elias walked to a large stone altar. "Take care and watch my son. You will need to know this for they will always hate you. They will never understand."

Israel watched with rapt fascination as his father knelt before the stone, adorned with symbols and etchings from a long forgotten past. Elias spoke, "I call upon the pact upon which my name lies. I call upon the bargain unbroken."

A great voice echoed through the chamber. "We honor the pact." From a pit, a glow of orange and yellow grew to an overpowering intensity. "Throw them in," the voice instructed.

Elias turned to Angeline, out of the folds of her night cloak she pulled out several handmade dolls like the one she wore about her neck. Angeline laughed as she walked to the pit and tossed the dolls in. She spat after them into the flames below.

The villagers were approaching the house when a wall of flame rose in front of them. It moved and licked at the shrubs and trees forming a barrier between them. Then it started to move.

It came toward them. As they turned and ran, it followed them. Then, it attacked them. Fingers of flame reached out and touched them one by one, and one by one they ignited. One by one they screamed and died, immolated to ash and bone shards. The fire extinguished itself, its purpose done.

Below the house in the chamber, the voice once again spoke, "The pact is honored." Elias stood up from the altar. It was good to be a Blakely; he'd made sure of that.

Behind was left a circle of scorched earth that never healed. The house on Blakely Hill still stands. Another generation occupies it.

Mikel B. Classen has been writing about northern Michigan in newspapers and magazines for over thirty-five years, creating feature articles about the history, travel, outdoors, and culture of Michigan's North Country. A journalist, historian, photographer, and author with a fascination of the world around him, he enjoys researching and writing about lost stories from the past. Classen makes his home in the oldest city in Michigan, the historic Sault Ste. Marie. He is also a collector of out-of-print history books, historical photographs, and prints of Upper Michigan. At Northern Michigan University, he studied English, history, journalism and photography. He lives with his wife, Mary L. Underwood, and his Labrador retriever, Grand Sable Dune. His book, *Au Sable Point Lighthouse, Beacon on Lake Superior's Shipwreck Coast*, was published in 2014 and his book, *Teddy Roosevelt and the Marquette Libel Trial*, was published in 2015, both by the History Press. He has two books of fiction called *Lake Superior Tales* and *Journeys into the Macabre*, both published by NetBound Books. To learn more about Mikel B. Classen and to see more of his work, check out his website http://www.mikelclassen.com.

Engraving - Indian Village

Iced

by Lee Arten

Below a ruined logging camp,
two beaver ponds with otter slides.
His left boot cracked the ice on one.
He sloshed around afterward
thinking frostbite but, as long as he kept
    moving,
the boot's felt liner kept him warm
    enough.

A ravine pointing at the lake
beside a slick haul road.
The thought of it rode him
while he hunted the hardwoods.
He stepped into it as the light began to
    dim.

At the top, the cut was tight with downed
    birches,
and pines that leaned and dropped snow
down his neck.
It widened as he moved,
slowly, wind in his face.
The place felt ripe.
"No-one hunts here," he said
"they go on up."

He shifted his rifle.
Cleared snow off the scope.

A pond, iced over, spread in front of him.
He walked the left bank.
Brush clogged the slope,
pinching him against the pond, till,
his right boot cracked the ice.

The sound cracked back at him. A deer,
a buck no doubt, rose, crashing,
from the other side.
Left behind: only a sense of movement.
It was gone before he got his rifle up.

He cut back.
Hurried through the brush above the
    pond.
Traced the big tracks across two farm
    roads.
The snow beyond the second set of ruts,
told him the buck had begun to run
    again.
He stood waiting, expecting a shot
from someone, till dark fell around him.

After bouncing around the U.S. and some islands in the South Pacific, **Lee Arten** came home to the Copper Country. Since then, he has arranged things so he writes, hunts, fishes, and shoots (not always in that order). His articles have appeared in many newspapers and magazines. *Upland Almanac* and *Gray's Sporting Journal* have published his poetry. He is working on a novel and a book on grouse hunting.

Hoffentot Magic

by Roslyn Elena McGrath

Underneath your car is a very old house about three-and-a-quarter millimeters wide and half a millimeter high, home to a very large Hoffentot who has lived there since before time began.

When he was a very small Hoffentot, he lived underneath a shoe with his family of two parents, two siblings, and two very old, torn tomes on what a grown Hoffentot and a growing Hoffentot should do.

After he had read them both fourteen or fifteen times, he knew this was not the life for him, so he left his family and their surrounding Hoffentot village to strike out on his own.

The youthful Hoffentot traveled far and wide, experiencing new vistas, including places where no Hoffentot had gone before. He could always tell when this was the case, because there wouldn't be a speck of remains of a Hoffentot home or village, and all the area denizens, from old to young, would look at him in amazement.

But this bold young Hoffentot took it all in stride. "Well, someone's got to be first," he told himself, "So it may as well be me."

After three years and five days of this peripatetic life, our Hoffentot began to be a bit bored of traveling from place to place. He decided he'd like to settle in somewhere where he could practice his skills as a magician and wow the local folk.

And so he settled underneath your vehicle, which he is certain he makes disappear and reappear regularly.

Roslyn McGrath believes in the magic within all things. She translates her creative arts background and intuitive healing work into personal growth and inspiration books and meditation CDs. Roslyn is the author of *Goddess Heart Rising, Chakras Alive!* and *The Third Mary,* as well as the publisher of free quarterly *Health & Happiness U.P. Magazine.* Visit www.EmpoweringLightworks.com to see more of her offerings.

Lake Superior and Ishpeming Railroad steam engine

Ann Dallman

Wolf Woman

She runs with the wolves
The pack is at her side.

Braying at the moonlight
Daring to enter his home at night.

She yips at his heels
And nuzzles his sleeping form.

"Wake up, the moon is full,"
She calls to her former lover.

But he sleeps on, unaware
That he has lost the race, the adventure.

He is old, discouraged
He has deserted her. She runs alone.

Menominee County/ My Hometown Abandoned

An old bridge stands rusty
Witness to the passerby
As if to say—*Notice me, I'm here.*

Lumber barons and loggers
Once roamed our wooded land
And crossed the Menominee River.

They cut and hauled trees
And shot deer for sustenance
All in the name of survival's progress.

Years later the trees have grown back
The river flows heavily in spring
And freezes in winter.
The deer and black bear have replenished.

Only the bridge stands forsaken and alone.

A former English teacher, **Ann Dallman** edited, wrote, and did the graphic design for *Sam English: The Life, Work and Times of An Artist* (2009 Coffee Table Book of the Year/PEAK Award). She's received scholarships to Split Rock Arts Institute/Minnesota; Highlights Foundations sessions/ Pennsylvania and three writer's residences at Wild Acres Retreat Center/North Carolina. A former newspaper editor, she has also published in national trade magazines. The Society of Children's Book Writers and Illustrators/Michigan Chapter named her as Runner Up in its 2016 Multicultural Mentorship Competition.

Christine Saari

At Camp

Jon's boyhood boat sails in the rafters.
Grandmother's flour bin lives near the
    stove.
Deer skulls rest on the shelf by the window
Father's cuckoo clock does not tick any-
    more.

We have an outhouse under the hemlock.
Dishes are chipped. Pots full of dents.
We don't take off our shoes or wear slip-
    pers.
Our clothes come from the thrift shop in
    town.

Flowers bloom wild. The grass grows high.
We pick raspberries for breakfast.
We hunt for mushrooms after a rain.
Our water flows from a spring in the forest.

Mice nest in the chest of drawers.
A pine snake lives under the deck.
Wild turkeys leave fathers on pathways.
Red squirrels gnaw through the logs.

We glide down the river in search of the
    beaver.
We wonder where the heron has gone.
The dipper stands high in the clearing.
The full moon shines onto our bed.

We read by the glow of oil lamps
And go to bed before dark.
We make wolf-howling love in the sleep loft
Under garlands of blooming wild hops.

At camp we dream, we putter, we play.
We leave the city behind, don't listen to
    news.
Here the past meets the present.
Our souls are restored. Time stands still.

Nonetheless

Someone dumped a toilet off the Diffin
    Road Bridge.
A dead calf once landed on the Whitefish
    River ice.
We fish for beer cans every time we canoe.
We hear traffic noise from the highway
    nearby.

Nonetheless: Muskrat, kingfisher, and wild
    turkey
Have made this stretch of stream their
    home.
We have watched a blue heron fish at our
    landing.
New cuttings let us know the beaver was
    here.
We have seen deer leap across the river.
Once a bear lumbered out of the forest,
    on to the road.

This is not wilderness. Nonetheless,
Animals rule here and we are privileged
    guests.

Christine Saari, writer and visual artist, grew up in Austria, immigrated to the USA in 1964 and has lived in the UP since 1971. The Saaris own a rustic camp on the Whitefish River and are active in conservation issues. Her publications include: *Love and War at Stag Farm, the story of an Austrian mountain farm, 1938-1948* (Memoir), "Christmas 1943", Silver Birch Press (poem), "Ten Days before He Died," *Water Music*, Great Lakes States Poetry Anthology (poem), and photographs and journalistic writing (US/ Austria).

Katydids

by Aimée Bissonette

It's a hot summer night in mid-July.
The air is heavy and the moon is high.
And it seems like the time
for a girl and a guy
katydid
to meet in the middle
of the great leafy branches of the thick tall tree
where the light and the shadow do-si-do in the breeze
and our katy-dating friends chew on tasty katy leaves
and get to know one another
just a little.
Our katy fella, he is smitten, thumps his leg and croons.
Scrapes one wing o'er the other, strums some katy-diddle tunes.
And our katy little lady, well she downright swoons.
Serenaded by his
katy-diddle fiddle.
Then the other katydids in the lush canopy
strum and thrum all as one,
a katyfiddle symphony.
And the chorus swells around them. Buzzes, ticks, and rasps surround them.
Til they think the sound will drown them.
What a racket! What a fright!
What a katydiddle cluster
on a hot summer night.

Aimée Bissonette splits her time between her home in Minneapolis and Copper Harbor, Michigan. She has two published picture books: *North Woods Girl* (Minnesota Historical Society Press 2015 – Sigurd Olson Nature Writing Award; Midwest Booksellers Choice Award; Friends of America`n Writers Award and *Miss Colfax's Light* (Sleeping Bear Press 2016). She is currently working on another picture book with Sleeping Bear Press. For more information, go to www.aimeebissonette.com.

The artist is Claudia McGehee, who illustrated Aimee's first picture book, *North Woods Girl*. Her email address is cmc@claudia-mcgehee.com. Her website is http://www.claudia-mcgehee.com.

Source

by Frank Farwell

Even though it's been more than 27 years, I still can't believe it's really over; not a week goes by that I don't think of her and our journey. Sometimes I awake, sweating and trembling, at 3 a.m. from some nightmare of deadlines and the difficulties with Communist China in the old days of the early 1980s.

But it must truly be done with, because looking through my tent screen at the dying campfire and watching a cold, clear sky full of stars on this spectacular night, well, I feel real freedom. There is no feeling like it—especially when a person is up here on the Canadian edge of the big, magical lake, in the richest cradle of boreal forest and granite-studded coast between Labrador and Alaska's Glacier Bay. I savor every minute, breathing in the sweetness of cedar and balsam by the shore of the inland sea.

The truth is, when I say "she," I am referring to my former business. It's thanks to her that I'm no longer living paycheck to paycheck in a crowded city, and am free to be living up here in the woods outside Marquette.

Now, you might think that talking about a business is a stupid thing to do when I'm unshaven and happy, just me and my canoe under the cloud-dusted cold belly of a northern night sky, where stars peep out of the gathering clear blackness of another world like tiny silver candy on a dark chocolate cake. And you'd be right.

Except for this: While a small business may grow and eventually give its founder and owner the time and resources to transition into a coveted new life, close to 95 percent of new business startups fail within the first

10 years, according to the statistical geeks at the U.S. Small Business Administration. The winner's circle is an elusive 5 percent, yet it's these few survivors in cities, suburbs and rural America who create most new jobs and economic growth.

Despite these slim odds, entrepreneurs keep jumping off the cliffs of job security like a bunch of intoxicated lemmings, expecting to find some new elixir in the sea below. Usually only unforgiving rocks await them at the bottom of those cliffs. Even so, these leaps for freedom create new businesses like nothing else. It must be the human spirit's inner soul, desperate to get out of the eternal prison of working for someone else, desperately seeking freedom via self-employment.

Back in 1979, I too wanted out—of the grinding routine of commuting to and from New York City's big company employment, that is. I needed to cut loose emotionally, sociologically, the whole enchilada. I had heard about the 95 percent failure rate but, damn, I didn't want some statistician's number standing in my way. So I just ignored it.

Clueless, I too took the leap. I sold my house, borrowed against it, moved back to the Midwest, and the adventure began. It was a rough ride in the early years; there wasn't a bonehead blunder I didn't make. But, things got figured out, and after the 11th year, I sold my business to a Wall Street investment firm and, well, now my family lives near the most magical lake of them all—Superior, the giant, clear gift of an inland sea. There is hardly a better place to sail, paddle, cross-country ski, or raise a child.

Anyway, it is dusk in early September in northern Ontario as my canoe coasts into the shelter of a deep, narrow cove. Five minutes later, a female calf moose ambles out of the woods, 100 feet away, and stands knee-deep in the shallows, eating plants off the bottom. Then she sees me and freezes. A minute later, a large bull moose with a huge set of antlers thunders out of the woods, notices me, and starts walking closer. I strip things out of the canoe to lighten the load, grab a paddle, and get ready to make a fast exit. The moose stops 100 feet away, perhaps realizing I'm not interested in his lady friend.

As the campfire dies two hours later, I start to doze off and head for my tent and a warm sleeping bag. In the morning, a caribou with an elegant silver mane struts down to drink from the pristine, shallow bay. He stays a few moments, 150 feet away, and then ambles off through the bush. I'm an imposter in his world.

A while later, I pack up camp and paddle east into a cold headwind, staying close to shore. Rain begins, and the darkened sky causes the lake to turn from clear blue and green to silver gray. After four hours of hard paddling, the sky brightens and a river comes thundering out of a crevice in the granite hills and cascades down three staircase waterfalls, the last of which plunges 30 feet into the lake with a deafening roar. I slide up close so my bow almost touches the torrent and sit still for a moment, feeling the water thundering a few feet before me. The small, rocky beach next to it is an exquisite place for a campsite.

The next morning, after a two-mile crossing to an outer island, I stop to bob in leftover swells, looking up at a lighthouse perched high on top of the western end of the rocky island. Through the 1970s, before the stations were solar-automated, light keepers from the Canadian Coast Guard lived here April to November and might not see anybody for weeks at a time. If you showed up in a leaky wood canoe, bristle-cheeked, smelling of campfire smoke and badly in need of a bath, you were just about a prodigal son returning home, and welcomed with a feast of canned goods, fresh bread, and lake trout. Now the lighthouse is deserted, automatic, sterile.

The sterility fills me with an emptiness; I miss the light keepers, whom I had met on earlier trips. Two German hikers I encountered in Oiseau Bay three days ago were the first and last people I have seen on this trip. There are no other humans for 35 miles to the west, east, or north, and 150 miles to the south. I welcome the stark loneliness, but miss the mini-village that was the lighthouse.

I make camp on the leeward side of the island, and when it's nearly dark, paddle to its western tip, moving slowly in three-foot swells and the resultant backwash off the rocky shoreline. Waves break over a reef to my right. The gold and silver of the fading sun ebb into orange and then a darkening charcoal gray. There is a deep joy in being here, floating magically on the desolate water's surge.

When Étienne Brûlé, the first visiting white man, came upon Lake Superior, in 1666, he wrote in his journal: "A true inland, fresh water ocean without tides." To succeeding generations of voyageurs, fur traders, trappers, and now modern-day wilderness paddlers, it's a spellbinding presence. It's exactly that for me as night brings wind, rain, a leaky tent.

A strong breeze builds, and at dawn eases, leaving a fog that envelops everything in miniscule water pellets. Cobwebs left by summer spiders are laced with droplets that glimmer like tiny diamonds. In mid-morning my canoe transits quietly eastward off the south shore of the island, while a garden of rocks beams up from the bottom 5, 10, and 12 feet below in shades of rust red, green, granite gray, white and pink.

Rounding a small point, I surprise a loon napping, just offshore. He jerks his head up and looks at me as if I were a creature from another planet, which to him I'm sure I am in my orange life jacket, yellow rain gear, light green spray skirt stretched tightly over the canoe, and bright blue rubber packs. He paddles madly with his feet and then takes off.

Nowadays, tourists come to the west edge of Puckaskwa National Park, where I began my trip, and steer their cars and vans to the government campsite. Some walk the half-mile trail around rocky overlooks, peer up and down the coast, and then continue back to their campers, pack up the next morning, and head west toward Thunder Bay, and on to Winnipeg, or turn south at Thunder Bay toward Duluth. For a continent whose interior was first explored and developed by canoe and on foot, we've become a sorry, soft lot—all the while having cleansed the wilderness of its native populations.

Moss, spruce, cedar, balsam, white pine and birch cover the island to the water's edge, making the occasional granite edges seem to erupt out of the woods. I glide over a shallow rock garden of colored, ancient small boulders that shimmer from a patch of sand bottom 6 feet below, like a kaleidoscope of evolution. The rocks are all different—like the people one has for friends or family or work associates—yet somehow they all fit together, like a puzzle.

The loon calls out on my left and starts swimming out of the fog toward me. At 40 feet he calls again, perhaps disappointed there is no reply from the strange creature in the boat. I feebly attempt a loon call, and he turns and cocks his head sideways as if to say, "What the heck was that?"

He holds his distance, paddling with his feet in a semi-circle around one side of the canoe, and watches me continue down the bay, back into the fog. His species has lived exactly in its same life form for five million years. Compared to loons, humans are a failed modern innovation.

At the end of the island, I stand in the shallows and fill water bottles from the lake's chill, clear waters. My compass has a mirror panel for emergency signaling, and leaning forward I get a glimpse of myself. If someone looking like me showed up for a job interview, I would call the police.

Paddling past the eastern tip of the island, out into the foggy strait, a leftover swell comes in from the open lake. It feels like a living, liquid force that has gone on forever, and carries me effortlessly along. Another 30 minutes paddling north and the dull outline of the mainland shore slowly becomes visible. Soon the mid-day heat above the fog

opens visibility to a quarter mile, and around a bend in the shoreline I see the framework of an old trapper's cabin. It has a decrepit, rock-anchored dock, and as if to mock the passage of time, two families of beaver have built lodges amidst the dock's remains. Nature has the last laugh.

I paddle under cliffs toward the end of a long cove, make camp, and at nightfall stars shine brightly in a clear quadrant of sky. While I'm brushing my teeth at the water's edge, a beaver swims by in the moonlight, leaving a V-wake like a small battleship. Fish sporadically rise out of the water, dining on surface bugs. Later, a skunk meanders through my campsite, irritated to find me on his turf. A shooting star zooms high overhead, igniting and burning out in four seconds. A satellite hurtles through space. What I guess is a heron flies by with slow wing movements in the dark, its wings flapping 20 feet above the shoreline. A white-throated sparrow calls its song until about 9 p.m., and then packs it in for the night.

Heavy footsteps splash in the dark on the opposite shore of the cove, probably a moose or caribou. A loon calls once, then stops. I hear another moose browsing on the weeds on the near shoreline and feel the earth shake as he climbs up the bank and nears my campsite. From inside my tent, his ponderous breathing sounds like lungs the size of a 55-gallon fuel drum. So ends day 7.

By morning it is cloudy again and blowing hard from the west; my scheduled float-plane pickup cannot land. By now, "tomorrow" seems more like a vague concept than a numbered box within a calendar.

The windy day passes and again the sun goes down in a spectacular chorus of red and orange to the west, in the direction of Isle Royale. Toward 11 p.m. the wind increases and gusts to 30 miles per hour, ripping savagely through the trees. They bend and creak as if calling to each other.

By midnight, with the moon obscured, the wind gusts to 35 m.p.h., then 40 or more. A pristine world shrieks around me as my tent shivers in the wind, and I drift off to sleep. In the moment before entering deep slumber I feel as if my spirit has come home; there is nowhere else I want to be. I know that, come morning, I will not want to leave. I want to freeze this moment in time and bury it deeply and safely in my unavoidably modern soul.

That trip was in 1992. I moved to Marquette, after 26 years in southern Wisconsin, in 2006, happy to be near the big lake's south shore, where I had so many happy childhood memories. Even so, it was the north shore of Superior I always wanted to return to, always needed to go back to. Without consistent doses of it, I could not feel centered, connected, or whole.

Time ebbed inexorably as the demands of everyday life dissipated the years. Some winter days, at dusk, I looked through our windows and saw the wind working its magic in the swaying bare treetops outside, reminding me of the forests, and its rocks, and quiet emerald coves of the north shore.

And so today, in early December, on my 66th birthday, I make plans to go back. It will be a less vigorous trip than the first one in 1973, and the most recent one in 1997, or the many in between, all of which ranged from 45 to 115 miles. It will still be a wooden canoe on open water, paddled solo along the edge of the inland sea, blessedly alone, far from nowhere, stripped to simplicity and thus connecting with self, origins, and spirit.

When I launch early next summer at Hattie Cove and paddle around the first headland to the east, toward deep wilderness, I know I will feel the quiet, nourishing surge of the silver-blue fresh water beneath me and the boiling, monstrous energy of the big rivers that pour through rocky canyons into the lake from the north. I know I will once again be younger, more alive than ever.

All winter I dream of that moment, like a hungry dog waiting for its dinner.

Frank Farwell was a newspaper reporter and magazine editor in New York until 1979, when he left to start a small business that grew to become a three-time INC. 500 company. Eleven years later the business, WinterSilks, was sold to a Wall Street investment firm. His book, *Chicken Lips: An Entrepreneur's Wild Adventures on the New Silk Road*, was an initial nominee for the 2011 Financial Times/Goldman Sachs Best Business Book of the Year award. His freelance work has appeared in the *New York Times* and numerous other publications. Frank can be reached at farwellf@gmail.com.

Jack LaPete, Marquette engraving

MEMBER BENEFITS:

Your Invitation to join the UPPAA Today

- Network with more than one hundred members of the publishing community
- Attend publishing/writing conferences and meetings
- Meet experts in the publishing industry!
- Receive the quarterly UPPAA newsletter, *The Written Word*
- Get discounts on IBPA and APSS Publisher Association Memberships
- Participate in the UPPAA email group for answers to all those publishing and marketing questions
- List your books & book covers at www.uppaa.org
- Display books at UPPAA tables at UPPAA meetings & other UP book events
- Learn the do's and don'ts of self-publishing
- Receive notice of upcoming book contests and awards
- Submit work for publication to the annual UP Reader magazine

Join now at http://uppaa.org/join-or-renew/

WHAT IS UPPAA?

UPPAA is the Upper Peninsula Publishers and Authors Association.

WHEN WAS UPPAA FOUNDED?

- The organization began in 1998 when Sue Robishaw, wishing to share her self-publishing experiences and learn from others, had the idea to form UPPAA. With the help of Lynn Emerick and Michael Marsden, the first UPPAA Conference was held in June 1998 at Northern Michigan University with thirty people in attendance.
- Since the organization's founding, UPPAA has grown to more than 100 members, representing a diverse body of writers in the fields of fiction, nonfiction, history, children's books, science and many other fields. You can view our members' books at www.uppaa.org.

WHAT IS UPPAA'S PURPOSE?

UPPAA was founded with the purpose to support and encourage networking and idea exchange among Upper Peninsula, and surrounding area, publishers and authors, and to promote books published and/or authored by UPPAA members.

DOES UPPAA HAVE MEETINGS?

- An annual conference is held in the spring and regular monthly meetings are also held. The meetings are held centrally in Marquette to provide convenience to members throughout the vast peninsula.
- The conference is usually divided into several workshops, focusing on such topics as writing, the mechanics of publishing, publishing cost-effectively, marketing, and publicity. UPPAA has also brought in internationally known guest speakers to its conferences, including Dan Poynter, Patrick Snow, Jerry Simmons, and Irene Watson.
- Attendance at conferences is free to UPPAA members.

HOW IS UPPAA ORGANIZED?

UPPAA is a non-profit organization with a Board of Directors. Board positions are open to any members and board members are nominated and voted in every two years by members.

WHAT IS UPPAA'S FUTURE?

With a group of enthusiastic and innovative members, UPPAA continues to grow and seek new ways in the rapidly changing world of book publishing to promote its Upper Michigan authors and their books.

A Tribute to Dad

by Sharon M. Kennedy

It's been thirty-one years since we lost Dad. Don't believe them when they tell you one year is enough to mourn, for mourning is nothing compared to the remembering. The remembering and longing never go away, they just creep into a far corner of your mind and wait until you grab an old shirt hanging on a rusty nail or slip into a pair of big rubber boots. Then it all comes back, even to the familiar scent of Lifebuoy on a scrubbed neck or the honk of a Sunday morning horn saying, "Hurry up or we'll be late for church."

I see Dad everywhere. I see him on the tractor as he plows the fields or in the barn as he milks the cows. But his fields are wild and overgrown now and the barn is falling down; but yet it, too, waits for Silver and Maude and all the other cows. There's evidence of you everywhere, dearest Dad, from the handmade chop boxes worn smooth by the cows, to the wire wrapped around the gate post. Shaky at best, but adequate enough to keep the cows from wandering.

The chicken coop caved in years ago, but I remember when I used to run and check for eggs. The coop always frightened me because it was low and dark, and I was afraid a hen might be setting and peck me. I remember the time a tomato plant grew outside the henhouse door, and I didn't want to pick the tomatoes because of where the seed had probably been; but you, dear Dad, laughed and popped a ripe tomato into your mouth. "Best tomato I've ever tasted," you said. Then there was the time you ordered hen chicks and when they were older, they turned into roosters and chased me from the barn to the house. You scooped me up and held me close as you kept the traitors at bay.

I remember the summer I came home, the summer I spent waiting. I don't know what I was waiting for, but it was enough merely to wait in languid anticipation of better days to come and you did not ask questions. Detroit faded into a whirlwind kaleidoscope behind me as I crossed the Mackinac Bridge and home beckoned. I returned to you and Mom and the farm where I lived my childhood. I returned to wait and, perhaps, to hope.

I was thirty then, had just turned thirty, and maybe that had something to do with it. Who can explain the mysterious longing to return to a birthplace, to loved parents? Not I, certainly not I. Not then, not now, but I remember that summer as if it were yesterday. Everyone said I was a fool; that I would return to the city within a week; that I would find things changed and be disappointed. Friends wagged fingers and said vacation there, don't move there. They preached and admonished and counseled, but I did not hear. How can one hear words of caution when memories whisper until they shout, "Come home, come home." I was blind, deaf, and heedless of everything except the need to return.

I found things much as I had left them. I breathed the stuff that had made me what I was, who I am. It was all there. Nothing had changed. Even the endless dust filling my car carried an aroma all its own, and I knew just as surely as I knew I lived and breathed that I was home.

Mom and you were there, smaller than I remembered, more weathered, more gray, but joyous. You walked with a cane now, not a real cane, but some heavy old tree branch you had worn smooth, and you, like the old house, leaned to one side. You hobbled behind Mom, taking your time on the steps and keeping one hand on the railing. When I hugged you, I could have wept because you had grown old.

I walked around the farm and saw washtubs full of rainwater and piles of rusty junk iron you were going to find a use for one day. I saw fences that were constantly being repaired now resting on the ground and wondered how many times your hands pulled the wire tight and your fingers got caught on the barbs. I saw an antique cast iron tub that had been used as a water trough because the tub was handy and there wasn't any use for it in the house because there was no bathroom so why would we need a tub. I saw the old house, vacant and listing to one side like a great ship taking on water and wished with all my heart it had been fixed up and I was coming home to it instead of the trailer.

I remembered the winters of my youth. You carried water from the well-house to the barn when the ground was too icy for the cows to walk to the trough, and you always leaned your head against the cow's flank when you milked her. Sometimes I watched and wondered where you were. You seemed so far away. Once I thought I saw tears on your cheeks when you turned to me. I asked if you were crying, and you said no. I didn't believe you then any more than I believed you when Gram died and you stood at her coffin and the same phantom tears you denied were clearly visible.

Memories. They're everywhere and just when you think you're over them, well bam, you realize it's all a sham and you're not over anything. You long for just one more minute, one more second to curl your arms around your dad and tell him you love him. Just half a second. Just any time at all. Then you pull yourself together and get on with your work, work of any kind that will take your mind off the memories. And yet you can't help but look up and hold your head still, listening as in the distance you hear a cow bell ring on a warm summer morning and wonder if maybe, just maybe, Dad's heading the cows for home one more time, and you run to the barn, run past the heaps of junk, past the well-house, past the cat sunning itself, run until you jump the rotted fence and close your eyes and wait and wish with all your heart that you could see him just one more time.

Memories. Sometimes they're all that keep the living alive.

Sharon M. Kennedy of Brimley published her book *Life in a Tin Can*, a collection of stories from her newspaper columns. After teaching English Composition at the college level, Sharon returned to her real love. Writing stories that tug at your heartstrings or bring a smile to your lips is her hallmark. She can be reached at P.O. Box 215, Brimley, MI 49715 or https://www.facebook.com/LifeInATinCan

Ononegwud Resort, Neebish Island

Ar Schneller

Nightcrawlers

Bright lights
scare them away
low light is the best
we shake our flashlights
for dying beams
hunched over chilled yards
mud huts around holes
searching for crawlers
as big as baby snakes
more night travelers
daddy long legs
creepy spiders, black beetles,
sometimes a caterpillar

We search for slime shine
deep brown earthworms
barely moving when
connecting with mates
stuck together side by side
they glisten in the moonlight

Others seem clueless
but move fast from danger
grabbing quick, some rip in half
white slime covers our hands
worm coats smell like fish
grassy towels wipe hands clean
bait stores pay a penny a piece
copper cash, midnight harvest
cramped backs, cold hands
millions more escape death
　our night is over, we crawl home.

Her Skin

In front of a computer
with reading glasses on
skin pulled tightly
like overstretched Saran Wrap
only washing dishes soothed
her arthritic hands

observing dry skin
joints ache with each keystroke
stretched diamond shaped cells
shiny straight lines of skin
she stares at old hands
her first thought, lotion
hydrate paper thin skins
into juicy oranges

fingerprints, dry, cracked and
　white
with swirls in them
partitioned mini puzzle pieces
sections that don't belong
a lifetime of abuse, scratches,
burns, bruises, scars
half-polished nails, hangnails
tired working hands
ones that wrote love letters
put to bed without lotion
an orchard absent of fruit
no longer smells sweet

Champ

Eyes
swollen shut
tell the tragedy
our family
dog dead
an accident

a cold
wash rag
on my face
searing hot
tears defeat
the process

Sorrow drains
to my ears
he cries
next to me
his best friend
gone

his nightmare
cutting trees
it falls wrong
a yelp
then nothing
but guilt

Ar Schneller, a third-generation Yooper, lives along the shores of Lake Superior near Little Girl's Point. U.P. scenery, life experiences, and people inspire her poetry, writing, photography and art. She wrote a Nanowrimo novel in November called *Yooper Life*. Currently she creates copper jewelry at her Downtown Art Place Studio in Ironwood. Her creative life gets interrupted when a poem idea pops in her head and stops everything for a short time.

Check out her website: www.yooperlife.com. She can be reached at arleneschneller@gmail.com or (906) 364-0992.

Heartwood

by Rebecca Tavernini

The man across the river
It seems, is uprooting trees
with his Isuzu SUV.
Rhoh Rhoh Rhoh, the engine strains,
rocking the chained red pine.
Gas pedal pumped and released
like a bass drum beat.
Rhoh Rhoh Rhoh. It goes and goes.
Until the first give: a knuckle crack
through the bark's bast.

His dog barks and yaps,
until the trunk splits like a static cackle of lightning,
splinters like a skateboarder's wrist,
splices like a jolt that wakes you between dreams.

I put an old handsaw from the shed
to a young sugar maple bed.
Hoh Hoh Hoh, dammit my lungs labor,
slicing at angles on smooth gray calves.
Hoh Hoh Hoh, I pull and push to hear the crack.

Squirrels worry, spiders rain from the canopy.
The solid centers of trees, formed of mere water, air and light,
scream to each other across the river
with disinterested ducks.

Rebecca Tavernini grew up in the U.P. She is publications director at Northern Michigan University. She has been involved in editing such books as *Voice on the Water: Great Lakes Native America Now* and *Northern Border: History and Lore of Michigan's Upper Peninsula.* She writes poetry on a typewriter at camp.

Edzordzi Agbozo

Rewinding

Something knocks the roof
Of this house

I hear an owl cry
Its dirge, similar to the ones
I heard last year on the other shore

News came again
The humble king with arrogant hands
Tumbled one dusk from his throne
And the kingdom sang alleluia.
When the farmer chases mother goat from
    the cassava farm
Children must not rejoice too much
Mother goat always teaches kids the art of
    thievery
So children must not rejoice too much

On this side of the Atlantic
A baby lamb with an ancient fur and
    a hidden claw
Shook the House of Dreams from the
    delusion
So we now know we are still to cross the
    bar
We are still to mix snow and charcoal
Into one decorative statue
The Masai grandchild took up the state
    sword
And everyone sang alleluia
Everyone proclaimed a genuine blend of red
    oil and water
Soon, we realized,
We must not toast too soon

When the owl cries
Something knocks on this house
And on many other doors
Opening up for the embrace of the old order
Where the dog and the bone
Know their places

Final Welcome

Beyond death
awaits the joy-full-ness
the nothing-ness
for which we kissed fires
and behind these
a vast green pasture
some say it is paradise
others, it is rest beyond the river
for me
the silence gathered for us
while we shuffle our feet
within the fallen leaves
in the forest we know
the festive flute-voice
we could not hear
and the long sleep we denied
still behind these
all our generosities heaped up
our supplications that could not be
    accepted
and the angst we held in our souls

They all shall be at our welcome feast.

Edzordzi Agbozo is an emerging Ghanaian poet whose works have been widely anthologized in Africa, India, USA, and performed in Norway and Ghana, including at the state funeral of the late President J.E. Atta Mills of Ghana and at the poetry night series at Moholt, Trondheim, Norway. His poetry has been honored with mentions in long-lists in Uganda and Ghana, and won the University of Ghana Community Excellence Award in the category of Creative Arts in 2012, was 1st Runner up in the Harmattan Poetry Contest in 2015, and 2nd Runner Up in the Kofi Awoonor Literary Prize competition in 2016.

He blogs at http://edordzi.blogspot.com/. His twitter handle is @death_dies.

The Visitors

by Sarah Maurer

I lie awake and then walk the halls,
Peer at the kids as they sleep, a tangle of sheets, limbs, breaths.
A favorite blanket has fallen to the floor.
In the bathroom, I study my reflection.
Quick movements outside the window catch my attention:
A head bobs, turns back, and then advances.
First one, then another, and another.
Their legs dip into the snow like wicks in hot wax,
Their noses, too: down in the snow, and then up, watching.
One is the most brave and rushes ahead.
The others follow
Pausing sometimes, circling each other, and then—
A leap!
A leap just for fun.
A fourth appears, the dawdler.
She (I believe it is a she) has kept to the shadows close to the trees.
But then all four move to the front of the house and I move with them,
Window to window,
Soundless as they,
Until they retreat.
Needle-like legs carry them back to the trees and shadows
And I return to bed
Still awake
But thankful for their visit.

Sara Maurer is a Sault Ste. Marie native who is married with two children. She works remotely for Comerica Bank as an operations analyst and writes poetry when not calculating key performance indicators. You can reach her at sshunk@albion.edu.

Active Dreams

by Sharon Marie Brunner

Briana tossed and turned on the powder blue satin sheets of her large four-poster bed as she drifted off into a deep slumber. There was a full moon and the moonlight illuminated the bedroom, casting shadows on the walls as the light breeze moved tree branches outside the window. Briana walked from room to room as if she was trying to locate something she lost. The back door of her home was opened and she walked into the back yard. The leaves made a crunching sound as her bare feet walked upon them. Her eyes were open wide as she stared at the path leading her further and further into the woods. She heard a sound behind her and she turned to look for the cause of the sound. Terror struck her and she began running as fast as she could. An embankment took her by surprise and she tumbled down the hill and landed by a large boulder.

Rays of moonlight streamed down through the tall pine trees in the woods. She was struggling against the ropes binding her wrists, waist, and ankles. Wolves were circling looking hungrily at her. The alpha male was getting closer and closer as he circled the tree. Screams were emanating silently in her head as she tried desperately to appear threatening to the predators.

She succumbed to the possibility of her impending death and was hoping for a quick death, void of as much pain as possible. The alpha wolf was getting closer and closer. Drool could be seen at the corner of his mouth as he made a huffing sound and started pawing the ground in front of Briana. The other wolves growled loudly awaiting their turn.

Suddenly Briana heard the galloping of a horse off in the distance. The wolves turned their heads toward the intrusion. She began screaming at the top of her lungs. A rifle was fired and a man's voice was heard shouting reassurances to her. A horse with its rider appeared in the clearing where she was held captive. The man aimed his rifle toward the wolves and fired. One of the wolves was hit and fell to the ground. The other wolves ran off into the woods. He jumped off his horse and ran to her. His black hair, bronze skin, blue eyes, and dazzling smile mesmerized Briana. His black vest strained against his muscular chest.

Her rescuer bent down and cut the ropes binding her to the tree. Being tied to the tree in the sitting position without food and water, along with the fear Briana faced washed over her. She collapsed on the ground in a heap at the stranger's feet.

The horse was pawing at the ground and whinnied nervously. The wolves hungrily approached the horse. Her rescuer aimed his rifle and shot toward the wolves, only missing the largest wolf by inches. The wolves ran off into the woods.

Briana was startled by the gun fire. She sprang to her feet shakily and planted her feet firmly on the ground to maintain her balance.

"Who are you? Where did you come from," asked Briana as she placed her hands on her hips, trying to hide her fear while looking intently into the stranger's eyes.

"My name is Brandon," responded the man as he smiled at her in his attempt to provide further comfort.

The image of the wolves devouring her defenseless body overtook her and she looked at her rescuer with fearful eyes.

"Don't worry, you're safe now," said Brandon as he cradled her in his arms tightly.

Briana melted in his embrace.

Brandon started licking her cheek.

She woke to her Scottish Terrier, Buddy, licking her cheek.

She examined her nightgown. It was tattered and dirty. Her feet were caked with dirt and her long, thick, auburn hair was strewn wildly about her head.

How did I get so dirty? Was I actually tied to that tree with those wolves circling me? Was that man or anything else in my dream real?

Briana quivered and pulled the covers up to her chin watching the shadows dancing across the ceiling as the trees swayed in the wind outside her bedroom window.

•••

Briana heard wolves howling off in the distance. The air was chilly for a fall day. Briana quickly jumped out of bed and slammed the windows shut and locked them. The window frames rattled as she did so. Briana stood shaking fiercely. She hugged herself and found a large sweater to cover her shoulders. Alone and afraid except for the company of Buddy, she tiptoed out of her bedroom. Even though daylight was breaking through the clouds, she clicked on the lights as she walked from room to room. Buddy tagged closely by her side. She felt even more disturbed when she discovered the kitchen door to her back yard was wide open. When she looked down at the floor she discovered muddy foot prints that led from the open door to the living room and into her bedroom.

Briana stood alongside the footprint and placed her foot aside one of the traces of evidence of the evening's escapades. The footprint matched the shape and size of her foot. Shivers ran down her spine as she realized she did not spend the entire night in her bed.

Where was I? I can't believe I'm here right now, looking at my own muddy footprints. Look at the shape I'm in. What's happening to me? Thought Briana as she hugged herself again to provide what little comfort afforded her.

Briana collapsed on one of her kitchen chairs and placed her head in her hands and began crying. The details from her dream were running through her mind. She remembered running from something or someone and being tied to the tree. She couldn't remember who the culprit was. Briana scratched her head, trying to remember. She was thankful she was saved just in time. Briana realized her dream may have been a reality and the wolves definitely posed a threat. Her thoughts quickly switched to the man who saved her.

That man was so handsome. Am I lonely? Is that my problem? Am I so busy during the day that I'm subconsciously seeking out a partner in my dreams? I have to provide some insurance that I stay in my home tonight and not go wandering in the woods again. I think I will put extra locks up high or maybe my friend Sally can stay with me. I will have to ensure my safety, from what, I wish I knew. What monster tied me to that tree?

She decided to put the events of the past evening behind her and get on with her day.

I have to get ready for work. It's French and German cuisine, the cuisines of choice for this week. Yes, I am in charge of my life, she told herself reassuringly. I can't wait to see the expressions on my customers' faces. The grand opening of Briana's international café was going to be held in only a few hours.

She took a leisurely shower and dressed in a French *maître d'* costume, which included a black tux complete with tails. Her crisp white shirt was topped off with a black bowtie. The black, pointed toe, leather shoes with a two inch heel completed the ensemble. Briana pulled her hair into a bun on the top of her head. Her oval face and large almond-shaped eyes added to the ambience of her attire. She put on a splash of brown eye shadow on her eyelids and then looked in the mirror to make sure she was ready to greet the day. Briana turned around to look at the tux she was wearing in her full-length mirror. She approved of the way she looked.

The day was laced with rays of sunshine peeping through the clouds and the dew was slowly drying on the grass. Mrs. Harvel waved at Briana while she was picking up the newspaper that was thrown by her front porch.

I hope Mrs. Harvel shows up at my open house today. She said she would. I wonder when Mr. Harvel is going to come back from his fishing trip with his cousin Morrie. Mrs. Harvel seems a little lonely without her husband.

"When's that husband of yours coming home?" asked Briana.

"Not until Friday," replied Mrs. Harvel.

Part of Briana's training when she was a child was to refer to people who were older than her by their salutation and last name. Her parents managed a retirement home for elders and when she was a child, she spent a lot of time with the elders at the center.

Briana returned her attention to the newspaper laid out in front of her on the kitchen table. She noticed there was a woman found dead in the woods and it appeared she was attacked by wild animals. The name of the woman was Savannah Smolinski.

•••

Briana arrived at the café. She eased her car into the small parking space behind the café and proceeded to the back door. The door was unlocked she discovered as she turned the knob. She walked in the back entrance and discovered Desiree, one of the cooks, kneading dough on a floured surface of one of the counters. Rock music was playing quietly in the background.

Briana got to work with the rest of the staff to prepare for the day. Everything was in order. The tables were set with deep crimson vinyl table cloths and black paper napkins were wrapped around silverware and set on each table. Deep green ceramic tiles covered the floors and the tiles were sparkling clean. The surfaces of the counters and glass were sparkling. The dining area was warm and welcoming with various themes illustrating the different ethnic foods that were going to be featured at the café hung on the walls.

Before the doors to the café were opened for business, all of the staff gathered in a circle with Briana as part of the circle. She decided to treat her staff like a team and asked them to put their fists in a circle with her hand on top of their hands and she said, "Let's go team." Everybody was beaming with excitement and trepidation, which was usually a part of the first day jitters for any business. Briana could feel her enthusiasm rising as she walked to the front door and turned the Closed sign to Open. Customers were already leaving their cars and approaching the café.

I am so glad I hired the Blue Point Advertising Agency to help me promote the grand opening of my new café. I saw ads on television and heard them on the radio. When I read the paper this morning, I saw the big spread in the paper. Nice work, Briana. I think this business of mine is going to be a success.

The first two customers to enter the café were the Harvels. Clarence Harvel decided to come home early to join his wife Henrietta when she came to the restaurant today. Henrietta was beaming as she held her husband's arm as he escorted her through the door and pulled out her chair for her to sit down. He was dressed in his fishing attire. Briana smiled and brought them menus.

"I see you decided to cut your trip short, Mr. Harvel, and by the look on Mrs. Harvel's face, she is glad you decided to come home early," said Briana as she smiled widely at the couple.

"Yes, the fishing wasn't going well and I would rather be in this lady's company instead of Morrie's any day," replied Mr. Harvel as he smiled at his wife.

"I tried to talk this beautiful wife of mine into coming with me this year and she told me that she wasn't going to miss your grand opening."

Briana sheepishly responded by saying, "I am so glad to have you as my neighbors."

Briana decided that the hours the café was going to be opened for business each day were from 11:00 a.m. to 7:00 p.m., six days a week and closed on Sundays. When her parents ran the home for the elderly, they had to work seven days a week and she felt everybody could use a day off each week to recharge their batteries. She stood by the front door of the café for most of the day and greeted customers as they entered. Each customer was given a chance to sign up for a drawing. One of the businesses she partnered with provided her a flat screen television and two desk lamps for the drawing at a reduced price.

The crepes, soufflés, and German sausages were a success. The rich French and German desserts displayed in the showcase were almost gone. The steady traffic kept all the staff busy but not overwhelmed.

Dusk was falling on the horizon. Briana turned to her staff and thanked them for such a great day of team work. She was impressed with herself for ordering enough food for the first day of business and about her food choices to serve to the customers. Many of the customers gave her compliments regarding the delicious food and wonderful service. She was glad to have the first day go so well.

"I am so proud of all of you. The food and service were wonderful. Do you have any recommendations concerning any changes you would like to see us make?" asked Briana.

The staff did not have any recommendations.

"I am going to get out of this monkey suit and help with cleaning," said Briana. She had packed jeans and a sweatshirt so she could clean in comfort. She entered the storage room to change her clothes. She patted herself on the back for a job well done.

All the staff and Briana began cleaning and putting things away. Much needed to be done before calling it a day.

A large red truck pulled up in front of the café. A man stepped out of the truck. From a distance he appeared to be tall and strikingly handsome. The staff and Briana were staring at the stranger as he neared the door of the café. As he opened the door, Briana suddenly realized she knew this man from somewhere.

Briana extended her hand to the stranger to welcome him as she introduced herself and told the man the café was closed for the evening.

He turned slowly to face Briana and gazed into to her eyes and said, "My name is Brandon." He smiled broadly at Briana.

Suddenly Briana realized this was the man who rescued her in her dream the previous evening. She began swaying from the uneasiness she was feeling. She collapsed in Brandon's arms.

Briana gazed into Brandon's blue eyes with awe as he returned her stare with a reassuring smile.

Sharon Brunner has written five books: *Shadow Travelers*, *Beyond the Shadows*, *Lake Superior in the Moonlight*, *Hidden Agendas: Beginnings*, and *Remnants of a Shattered Past: A Journey of Discovery and Hope*. All books are available on Amazon. Brunner has written many short stories and poems. Some of her poems were published by the Bayliss Library in a book of poetry. Brunner's blog is online at sharonbrunnerwrites. blogspot.com and her webpage at sharonbrunner.org. Brunner's email address is sbrunner4599@gmail.com.

Yachting on the Tahquamenon River